The Power and Impact of Courageous Changemakers: Stories of Life, Love, and Business offers a collection of moving stories that are a testament to the resilience, courage, and power of the human spirit. It's a beacon of inspiration urging us to be our own changemakers and, in turn, ignite transformation in the lives of others.

—Marci Shimoff, #1 *New York Times* bestselling author of *Happy for No Reason* and *Chicken Soup for the Woman's Soul*

Powerful and courageous! Openly sharing their personal experiences and passionate stories, the authors of *The Power and Impact of Courageous Changemakers: Stories of Life, Love, and Business* inspire you start your personal journey to a fulfilling life. Get ready to create new opportunities and possibilities, learning from the book's authors as they provide the tools and techniques they've used to overcome their personal challenges and improve their lives. I highly recommend you read it!

— Marilyn Alauria, intuitive life strategist

In a world where uncertainty and challenges often leave us feeling trapped, *The Power and Impact of Courageous Changemakers: Stories of Life, Love, and Business* is a flame of courage. It sparks the belief that change is not only possible but within our grasp, waiting to be embraced by those willing to take the leap.

If you are ready to break free from the shackles of circumstances, embrace change, and become a positive force in your life and the lives of others, this book is an invaluable companion. Grab your copy of *The Power and Impact of Courageous Changemakers* today and let the journey toward positive transformation begin!

—Mark Porteous, co-founder of the
Soul Affiliate Alliance

This book tells the experiences of ordinary people who faced times in their lives that presented frightening, difficult, even life-threatening situations. There are stories about challenges in business, communities, with families, and relationships. The accounts in this book show that you are not alone facing difficulties. The twenty-five authors openly share how they navigated their experiences to create new opportunities, mastery, and possibilities. You'll be inspired. *The Power and Impact of Courageous*

Changemakers: Stories of Life, Love, and Business will embolden you to become a brave changemaker, begin your next chapter, and tell your own impactful story. I recommend this book!

—Jodi Williams, Nobel Peace
Prize Laureate

Laughter heals! This book is packed with inspiring stories to encourage us all on the journey of healing and courageous changemaking.

—Craig Shoemaker, writer,
comedian, and actor

THE POWER AND IMPACT OF COURAGEOUS CHANGEMAKERS

Stories of Life, Love, and Business

Published by
Hybrid Global Publishing
333 E 14th Street
#3C
New York, NY 10003

Manufactured in the United States of America, or in the United Kingdom when distributed elsewhere.

DiDomenico, Donna.
Shalley, Sue
Courageous Changemakers
        ISBN: 978-1-961757-39-4
        eBook: 978-1-961757-40-0
        LCCN: 2024902025

Cover design by: Natasha Clawson
Mandala design by: Denise Sutter
Copyediting by: Claudia Volkman
Interior design by: Suba Murugan
Author photo by: Lauren Suchenski for Donna DiDomenico and Lennox Photography for Sue Shalley

courageousimpact.com

DEDICATION

This book is dedicated to current and future changemakers of the world.

CONTENTS

FOREWORD

We are The BoardRoom, a group of non-physical entities aligned for leadership and change. Donna is our voice, bringing our messages for inspired and brave leadership to leaders seeking to make a difference. We are all well-known leaders, US presidents, innovators, geniuses, and great inventors of the past.

We are honored Donna and Sue asked us to write the foreword of their book *The Power and Impact of Courageous Changemakers: Stories of Life, Love, and Business*. We are proud to speak of this book and of the twenty-five courageous authors who came together to make a difference in your life. They've opened their hearts to you by sharing their stories of triumph, challenge, and change.

We've been with Donna and Sue since they embarked on their journey. In the beginning, they were discouraged from writing their book. You see, they weren't famous. They didn't know any authors or have any contacts needed to create a book. They were told they would never bring the book to life.

Despite the negativity of others, they chose to keep going. They knew in their hearts this book would be a gift to all who read it. They set an intention for the book to be a reality. They knew there were twenty-five wonderful people, authors, who, like them, wanted to inspire others. They believed in their journey and had unwavering faith. They trusted the right authors would come to them. And they did!

Each author in the book has an amazing story and many lessons to share. Together, the authors' lights intertwine, creating a strong magnetic and powerful energy—one of love, peace, and compassion. You feel this special book's energy when you see, touch, and feel it. It's shared through the words, the pages, the cover of the book. The book empowers you to be different. You are propelled to act, to do something, as you are wrapped in the blanket of hope and faith created by the book.

The book's stories are enlightening, revealing, and insightful. The brave and compassionate authors expose their souls so you can benefit from their learnings. They want you to know you can change your life. They teach you to ask for what you want and to release what no longer serves you. Through their stories, you realize you are the changemaker in your life. You have the power to paint your future and make choices right for you.

The authors of *The Power and Impact of Courageous Changemakers: Stories of Life, Love, and Business* truly believe you are the creator of you.

Foreword

Whether it be in life, love, or business, you are the driver of your outcomes. Let their stories ignite your flame, take control, and live as you love. Remember, one step forward is all that is needed to start your journey. Let this book be the first step you take today as you become the changemaker in your life.

Feeling **your** love, faith, and joy **inside of you** are keys to fulfilling your vision and making changes you choose. Be open to your possibilities; accept and receive what is offered to you. Follow the breadcrumbs that mysteriously appear, as they form your roadmap to the life and fulfillment you desire.

Thank you to the gracious authors for baring your souls through your stories. We learned from you. You made us laugh, cry, cheer, and jeer as we rode the roller coaster of life with you. We praise your candor, your openness, your heartfelt sharing. We relate to you, as you, the authors, are ordinary people, humans, who want more for everyone.

There will always be hurdles and challenges. There is also always love, compassion, and hope. *The Power and Impact of Courageous Changemakers: Stories of Life, Love, and Business* is an example of how dreams become real when you have the faith and trust to believe in them. Donna and Sue prove this, as they've successfully published a book they were told they could never do.

—The BoardRoom

INTRODUCTION

The inspiration behind this book is to empower you to become your own changemaker and then to inspire other changemakers through your example.

Our motivation sprouted from observing people grappling with challenges, feeling trapped in their circumstances, and yearning for change without a clear path forward. In response to this need, we selected authors whose stories we knew would inspire you to think, act, and feel differently about what you're facing and ignite the flame of courage within to effect positive change.

Our Twenty-Five Authors

The Power and Influence of Courageous Changemakers: Stories of Life, Love, and Business features compelling narratives from twenty-five diverse authors who courageously share their stories, experiences, joys, and sorrows.

Our authors come from across the globe—Asia, Australia, Canada, and the United States. They are from different walks of life and range in age from thirty to eighty. However, the common thread running through each narrative is the willingness to make themselves vulnerable so you can learn from their experiences.

As you read their chapters, you'll find yourself chuckling, nodding with understanding, and reaching for a tissue during unexpectedly poignant moments. You'll admire each author's courage as they struggle with insurmountable challenges and applaud them as they face their deepest fears and triumph despite them. Above all else, you'll resonate with their journeys.

Written from the heart, they'll inspire you to take up the mantle and become a courageous changemaker. And if you'd like to connect with any of them for community and support, you'll find the author's contact information at the end of each chapter.

What's a Changemaker?

First, you need to know that changemakers are ordinary people navigating life much like anyone else. Many don't see themselves as changemakers because of their circumstances, yet deep within, they all hear the call to make a difference, even if they don't know how.

That's why this group of authors came together— to guide you. Their stories show how they responded to their call and will embolden you to face your fear with courage when you're ready to change.

Second, when one person makes a positive change for themselves, it creates a ripple effect, spreading outward and inspiring others to make similar changes, resonating far beyond that person's immediate environment.

In this way, one changemaker really can shape a future that is not only better but also more inclusive.

Mi Viaje es Tu Viaje

The book you hold isn't intended to be read once and then placed on a shelf to collect dust. It's meant to be a companion throughout your life's journey—a reliable source of inspiration and hope, ready to be revisited whenever needed. We expect it to be well-loved, oft-read, and shared widely with others.

Mi viaje es tu viaje are the words we use to describe this book—"my journey is your journey." And we consider ourselves to be *on* this and *in* this courageous life journey with you.

We look forward to seeing the changes you'll make in the world!

Donna DiDomenico
Sue Shalley

PRAYER
OF THE
CHANGEMAKER

Safire Rose

The dream that you carry in your heart is so close to you now.

> You can feel it in your bones.
> You can breathe it with your breath.
> You can touch it with your heartbeat.
> You can see it just ahead.

No one can tell you how to reach your goal
What steps to take, or what you should know.
And in those moments when you feel alone,
Call on the changemakers to carry you home.

Call on the changemakers to inspire and uplift.
Call on the changemakers to illuminate your gifts.

> Like Martin Luther King who had a living dream.
> Like Mohandas Ghandi who became the
> change he wanted to see.

Like Harriet Tubman who guided hundreds to be free.
Like Ruth Bader Ginsburg who set legal precedents notoriously.

Listen to the stories of those who have quickened inside.
In the middle of a moment,
In the twinkling of an eye.
Who did not give up when things went awry,
Throw in the towel, or say good-bye.

Who went beyond the conventions of the day.
Stepped out of the box and found a new way.
Redefined the hallmarks of worldly success.
And surrendered their fears to the river of change.

In the river of change you enter the unknown,
Let go of life's manual and create your own.
Release expectations of what you should do, and discover the importance of you being you.

With each bend in the curve, you must trust in the turn
That changes yourself and changes the world.
Rediscover what you knew all along
That you are the singer of your unique soul song.

Come out of the darkness
From behind the scenes.

Prayer of the Changemaker

Shine the light by your living,
By the heat of your dreams.

And when you know the truth of your soul,
There is nothing that can stop you,
You are in the flow.
And the river of surrender that seemed far away
Is yours for the taking, for the making of change.

For those who have inspired you by their words and
their ways,
Are now a part of you day by day.
Whatever the change, big or small;
When you change yourself deeply, you change us all.

Safire Rose, M.A., J.D., is a poet, author, teacher of timeless wisdom, and interspiritual minister. She is best known for her poem "She Let Go." Visit her website to learn about her upcoming book of poetry and free gift. Read her story later in this book.

Safire-Rose.com

MY ENTREPRENEURIAL JOURNEY FROM SCARCITY TO PROSPERITY

Sue Shalley

Knock, knock. A foreboding knock sounded on our company's door one day in January 2009.

When Alexandria, one of our employees, answered it, standing before her was a woman dressed in business casual—black slacks and a black blouse.

"May I help you?" Alexandria inquired.

"Yes, I'm from the Internal Revenue Service (IRS), and I need to see the proprietors of Field Services Unlimited. Are they available?"

Oh no! I'd heard that exchange from my office and knew precisely why the IRS was here. While Alexandria nodded her assent, I moved down the hall to intercept her.

"Hi," I said, "I'm one of the proprietors. My name is Sue Shalley. Come this way."

When we got to my office, she introduced herself and got straight to the point. "Mrs. Shalley, Field

Services Unlimited owes the IRS $141,000 in back taxes. Are you aware of that?"

I nodded.

"Can you write a check today for the total amount owed? Because if you can't, I'm here to close your business down."

I gulped, looked up, and saw, to my horror, our employees staring at me through the office windows. Wide-eyed with fear, they'd heard every word the IRS agent had spoken.

If this were a Star Trek episode, I would have flipped open my communicator and told Scotty to "beam me up!" Shame flared hot in my face as panic coursed through my veins. Desperation gripped my heart.

What was I going to do now?

Hoping for a Pickup

My husband, Bob, and I started our architectural services business in 1999. At the time, we were on the cutting edge, filling a need in the industry that few thought needed serving. Bob was the man in the field, and I was the CEO. Within ten years, we'd won contracts with national retailers, including H&R Block, Jack in the Box, Bank of America, ExxonMobil, and Starbucks. Our business was booming, and money was flowing.

Then, in 2008, our business started slowing down. It was the middle of the Great Recession in the United States, and the retailers we'd been working with weren't expanding or remodeling. Consequently, we struggled to find enough work to keep our staff employed and pay our bills.

We got behind on our taxes, and the IRS began sending us delinquency letters. At first, I ignored them, thinking the economy would pick up soon and there'd be money to pay the IRS.

It didn't and there wasn't.

Then, the IRS sent letters with bold red lettering across the top demanding immediate payment. That kicked me into gear, and I went to our tax attorney for advice.

Jim looked at our financial statement and said, "You're insolvent."

I burst into tears. How could this be? We'd been doing so well!

A Second Chance

Seeing the stricken look on my face, the IRS agent asked me about our business. She took notes as I talked about how our business had started, how long we'd been operating, our number of employees, who our clients were, and why we were behind in paying our taxes.

An hour later, she looked up and said, "Mrs. Shalley, here's what I'm going to do. I won't close your business down. You can keep your company name and continue doing business, but you must change your corporate structure and how you file taxes. And you'll need to enter into a payment agreement with us that includes past-due taxes, interest, and penalties."

I couldn't believe it!

Not only had Field Services Unlimited been given a second chance to catch up and continue, but so had I.

The Good Guys Never Get Ahead

My entrepreneurial journey didn't begin with Field Services Unlimited. And the roller coaster of scarcity to prosperity and back again didn't start with the Great Recession. It began around the dinner table.

Every evening when we sat down to eat, my father would look at his dinner plate, shake his head, and declare: "The good guys never get ahead."

When it came to prosperity, success, and money, this was my dad's truth. And all around me was evidence to that effect. Despite being the smartest person I knew, Dad always found himself underemployed and underpaid. He dropped out of college before graduating as a mechanical engineer and managed credit bureaus instead, spending his days tracking down individuals who couldn't or wouldn't pay their bills. This feeling of lack and evidence of no rewards for how hard Dad worked permeated our family.

While my parents were socially active, belonging to several clubs and having many friends with new cars, big houses, and mountain cabins, we struggled to keep up financially. My mother, adept at stretching dollars and skilled in sewing, knitting, cooking, and baking, worked tirelessly to create the illusion of equality. Still, my sister and I knew our dad wasn't as successful as other dads and our mom had to compensate for our lack of money.

As I grew older, I saw I wasn't the only one whose family lived on tight budgets. I wasn't the only one who longed to eat grocery-store Wonder Bread and Oreos and wear department-store clothes. From this environment of scarcity and pessimism, my entrepreneurial spirit was born. Unlike my father, I did want to get ahead. And I didn't want to make do with homemade clothes or home-baked bread.

I wanted to forge my path to success.

Embracing the Entrepreneurial Spirit

I had always wanted to try my hand at sales, so after college, I landed a job as a sales assistant selling luxury condominiums in Mexico. Next I helped grow the catering department at a high-end epicure retailer. My entrepreneurial spirit was taking flight.

When I returned to the United States, the entrepreneur flame within me burned bright. Together with my parents and sister, we started a catering business specializing in scratch baking, innovative menus, and events that exuded elegance and allure.

While outwardly successful, lurking beneath was the haunting echo of our father's truth. And despite how popular we were or how well we did, we never got ahead. My dad's belief that "the good guys never get ahead" infected us all, undermining our ability to assert the value of our products and charge what we deserved.

Snap Goes the Rubber Band

We remained ensnarled no matter how much we all tried to move past the conditioning of our father's truth and the reality of our living conditions growing up. It was as if an unseen rubber band had one end firmly rooted in the past, permitting us to stretch and evolve, but only to a certain extent. When progress seemed promising, the band would snap us back to the familiar grounds of pessimism and lack.

We stretched ourselves to the very limits of our metaphorical rubber band, and six years later, we had to close the doors. . . .

See, the good guys never get ahead.

Enduring Spirit

Yet, my entrepreneurial spirit endured.

In 1992, Bob worked for an engineering company conducting light-level readings at ATMs. He was the only one out in the field doing this unique assessment. And seven years later, Field Services Unlimited was born.

However, the invisible rubber band remained tethered in the past. And when the IRS knocked on our doors in 2009, we'd stretched the rubber band's elasticity to the limit. With a resounding *snap*, I faced the possibility that I'd have to close the doors of yet another business. This time, though, I stamped my foot and declared: "No! Not this time!" And I felt the anchor loosen.

Inner Journey/Outer Reality

With that one courageous act, I took control of my metaphorical rubber band. I boldly declared my truth and stood my ground. My end of the rubber band would no longer be attached to and dictated by the past. Instead, I anchored the end of my rubber band in the present and carved out a resolution with the IRS that paved the way to a prosperous future. My inner journey aligned with my outer reality for the first time, and I faced my future with steadfast determination.

Notes Along the Journey

Along my journey from scarcity to prosperity, I've learned that once you take control of your metaphorical rubber band and anchor it in the present, unlimited possibilities for expansion, growth, and prosperity open before you.

When you craft your narrative of success, you don't need to settle for less or accept past scripting of scarcity and lack. You can ask for more of anything you want, including more money.

So, dream big, ask for more, and express gratitude for what you receive. This is a mantra I repeat each day that I hope you'll find useful, too:

Thank you for the money in.
Thank you for the money out.
More, please!

The entrepreneurial spirit—the relentless pursuit of passion, the resilience in the face of setbacks, and the unwavering belief in one's value—is alive and well.

The good guys and gals do get ahead and prosper.

 Passionate entrepreneur **Sue Shalley**, with a thriving business development and marketing track record, founded a multimillion-dollar venture for Fortune 100 clients. As an insightful coach, she employs the CLASSY sales process, emphasizing prosperity through a "more please with ease" mindset, abundant gratitude, and joyful expectancy for entrepreneurs seeking fulfillment and success.

ProsperKindly.com

TAKE
THE
FIRST STEP

Anela Arcari

Flashback: I am standing in a wide-open space, entirely unprotected from the enemy. I am completely frozen in time and space—unable to take one step.

Where was I and how did I get there? I was in Somalia, in a combat zone where the lives of my soldiers were absolutely on the line—or so I believed in that moment. As their platoon leader, their lives depended on my decisions and my orders. They looked to me and the platoon sergeant to care for them and their families. It was an enormous responsibility and an incredible honor. Did I mention I was only twenty-four years old—in charge of thirty-eight soldiers and half a million dollars' worth of equipment?

While officially, it was a United Nations humanitarian mission, in three months we went from an average of three to five attacks against the UN forces to an average of thirty each week. This was the closest I'd ever come to combat during my twenty-eight-year career and the only time I wasn't sure I would come home alive. I genuinely feared for my life. So much so that I sat quietly one day reviewing my life and asking myself if I had any regrets. At that time in my young life, I only had one. I vowed if I made it out alive, I would reach out to that person and make amends, which I did.

On that particular day, a messenger came to my living area that also served as my office. He told me that the company commander needed to see all the platoon leaders immediately. The soldier explained there was a credible report that our base camp would be attacked by two hundred outraged Somalians. As the messenger left, I threw on the flak vest that had become my second skin. I then grabbed my weapon, an M16 rifle, and slung it over my back. Finally, I put on my Kevlar helmet, picked up my notebook, and headed out the door.

My door was about twenty-five steps from the door of our headquarters—an abandoned, rundown, looted home that happened to be painted white that we affectionately and sarcastically called "The White House." Not very original, but that's what it was.

The very short walk was across a completely open area; it was right in front of the main access point into our base camp—where the Somalians would soon be trying to gain entrance into our secured "safe haven." In my mind, I saw two hundred people climbing up and over the gate. I imagined that within minutes, we would be overrun by this angry mob.

I thought, *How will we defend against such an attack?* With that image and thought in my mind, I FROZE. I was about halfway between the two doors, and I stopped, unable to move in any direction.

My body's initial response was not fight-or-flight; it was to freeze in place and shake uncontrollably. I had never been this scared in my life! My nervous system was desperately trying to process the inconceivable image that filled my brain. I stood there for what seemed like minutes but was probably only a few seconds, thinking, *How will I take the first step?*

I was completely immobile; my feet would not budge. I was in the open, completely unprotected. Anyone in the buildings around our base camp could fire a weapon at me. One shot, and I would be hit and maybe even dead. Not even that thought jarred me. I simply couldn't will myself to put one foot in front of the other.

As my body continued to tremble, I began to feel nauseous as I once again imagined hordes of Somalians pouring over and through the gate. Internally, I reprimanded myself. I was screaming at myself to just take one step. I could not do it.

Then the next thought and vision came into my mind. Behind me in the building I had just walked out of were several of my soldiers. Without turning around, I saw them looking out the door and window at me, watching me. I knew instinctively they were waiting to see what my next action—literally my next step—would be. That image hit the back of my head like a two-by-four. I knew that for their sake, I had to find it in me to move as calmly as I could.

With that picture of them staring at my back, I found the courage to take the first step and then another. It took every ounce of bravery not to run to the door of "The White House." That would be a flight response—to run, run, run as fast as I could to safety, cover, and protection.

I knew that if I did that, I would only confirm their fears, and panic might spread like wildfire throughout the entire platoon. If I maintained a cool, collected, level head, then they would do the same. Leaders set the tone, always. While I had no idea how we would manage an attack of that size, I did know that all I had to do was get inside our headquarters. There I would receive the plan and my orders.

I appreciate that the challenges you face might not be in combat situations. I also know that no matter the circumstances, there will be something that causes you to stop in your tracks. The harder it is to take the first step, the more important it is for you to take it!

Taking the first step allows the second step to reveal itself. Taking the second step allows the third step, and before you know it, you have achieved a goal or a dream.

In my example, I found the nerve to take one step forward when every single cell in my body was shouting at me to do the opposite. Any journey or story begins with the first step and only unfolds in the present moment. The courage I gathered in that moment in Somalia stays with me today and inspires me when I feel I can't move forward.

Being a Courageous Changemaker takes intestinal fortitude. And it all begins with the first step!

On your path to becoming a Courageous Changemaker:

- Be clear on what will motivate you. Knowing my soldiers were watching me take my step motivated me.
- Don't worry about all the steps. Trying to figure out step twenty before you take step one may quickly overwhelm you.
- Taking step one with complete faith and intention that step two will show up allows you to see or receive an idea about that second step.
- Taking step two with complete faith and intention that step three will show up—you get the idea. Before you know it, you've completed step twenty.
- If you find yourself stuck, consider finding support by taking a course or working with a coach.

In my experience, the decision to keep taking first steps plays a vital role in becoming all I can be: a Courageous Changemaker. Each time I have taken a difficult first action step, it has led to personal inner growth.

May this chapter and book inspire you to take the first step and be a Courageous Changemaker. The world needs you and your light!

Anela Arcari is a combat engineer veteran with twenty-eight years of service turned intuitive, mystical coach. An Amazon bestselling contributing author and executive producer, Anela's innate gifts elicit the best transformation for her clients. Anela lives in Brooklyn, New York, and is a National Certified Counselor (NCC).

AnelaArcari.com

A VISION BEYOND LIMITATIONS: SEEING LIFE BEYOND GLASSES

Barry Auchettl

I have a vision of a future where our innate abilities, including sight, can overcome life's most daunting challenges—where the mind, body, and spirit's resilience converges to offer new perspectives. Imagine a future free from the reliance on glasses, contact lenses, or any external aid. In this envisioned future, it's about more than just seeing clearly; it's about perceiving our world through lenses unclouded by trauma, limitations, or fears.

In my early years, I walked the path carved out by my family's legacy—a world seen through the confines of eyeglasses. The revelation of my blurry vision emerged during a fleeting moment in high school when a friend's glasses became my temporary lens to the world. That moment paved the way for my own first pair of glasses.

While I actively played sports, my inability to see the ball's depth without glasses led me to believe I lacked talent. This blurry vision only worsened, and soon, I was wearing glasses almost every waking moment. Every two years, my visits to the optometrist resulted in stronger prescriptions. By my early thirties, I was using multifocal lenses, which were exceedingly stronger each time I upgraded.

But, as they say, every cloud has a silver lining. During a routine visit for my son, an optometrist introduced the possibility of eye exercises. Though my initial reaction was skepticism, a seed of curiosity was sown. If this stronger pair of glasses was my vision at thirty-two, what would I need by my forties or even fifties?

Fueled by a determination to redefine my sight, I embarked on a two-month self-experiment. Among the various exercises I practiced, *palming* was a revelation. The technique is deceptively simple, yet its transformative power cannot be overstated. As warmth flowed from my palms to my eyes, it felt as though they were being rejuvenated from within. The exercise became my daily ritual.

Here is the process I used for palming:

1. Sit comfortably, elbows rested on a table or desk.
2. Rub your hands vigorously until they're warm.
3. Close your eyes. Cup your hands, imagining holding a fragile egg inside each.

4. Gently place your cupped hands over your eyes. Feel the warmth of your hands.
5. Focus on your breathing. Let the mind wander without judgment.
6. Envision your hands' energy healing your eyes, breathing life into them.
7. After a couple of minutes, lower your hands. Gently massage the eye corners using your index and middle fingers for one or two seconds.
8. Open your eyes, embracing the newfound clarity and calmness.

The beauty of palming is its simplicity, yet its results can be profoundly transformative.

During this phase, an everyday incident underscored a profound realization: Our emotions are intrinsically linked to our vision. Without glasses, I went to get a spoon from the drawer and got angry when I thought I couldn't see it. I put my glasses on and watched the anger drain from my body.

With this realization, my journey took an upward turn. In just two months, my deteriorating eyesight plateaued, and remarkably, I returned to a simpler prescription for distance only. Emboldened by this progress, I set a lofty goal: to liberate myself from glasses within two years. I actually achieved this incredible milestone of 20/20 vision in just six months.

However, a follow-up appointment with the optometrist revealed a significant health concern—a pituitary tumor sitting on the optic nerve in my brain. I immediately underwent surgery, and the tumor was partially removed in order to save my life. I no longer saw life in the same way.

This diagnosis initiated a new journey, blending conventional medical understandings with holistic healing practices such as Reiki, kinesiology, and massage. Drawing from my own experiences and new skills, I started offering eyesight improvement classes. As my health found its balance, my vision became a beacon of hope, inspiring many.

A new curveball came four years later when further brain complications arose, leaving me with daily facial nerve pain. As a result, I was forced to leave classroom teaching and even collected on my full "death insurance" on the basis that I did not have much longer to live.

Instead of giving up, I stepped up and founded "Eye Power" to revolutionize how people perceive sight. I extended my vision teachings across Australia and New Zealand, emphasizing both physical eyesight and life's vision. My dedication led me to obtain a master's in education focusing on the detrimental effects computers have on eyesight and what can be done about it.

The nerve pain receded, and despite facing more surgery on the pituitary tumor in 2008, I continued my mission, relocating to the Gold Coast in Australia after my wife left me the same year. I was determined to start again because I believed that what I was doing was my soul's purpose, and I continued on this path of restoring eyesight and vision for others.

A few years later, I spoke at the Natural Vision Educators' conference in Los Angeles. I shared the symbiotic relationship between emotional intelligence and vision—that how we see is related to how we feel. This exploration was timely, considering the global rise in visual impairments affecting more that 50 percent of the population.

Stories of transformation, like that of a Canadian gentleman, John, fueled me to continue this path. John's journey stands out as a testament to the power of redefining one's vision. John had his eyes tested by an optometrist and then diligently worked through the ten-day program I gave him. then he went back to the optometrist to be retested.

He experienced such remarkable improvements in his vision that his optometrist was convinced he had undergone laser surgery. This striking transformation not only rekindled his hope but also underscored the potential for individuals to take control of their visual well-being. John's story serves as a shining example of how addressing the emotional and psychological aspects of vision, alongside physical practices, can lead to astonishing results, ultimately reshaping one's perception of what's possible in the realm of eyesight.

A year later, Eye Power became The Vision School in order to widen the scope of my vision work. I began focusing on the intricate dance between the internal vibration of how we see ourselves and the external frequency at which we perceive the world. Over the next several years, the business finally took off, and I was able to see a return on my years of hard work .

As our world continues to evolve, The Vision School addresses not just the symptomatic visual issues but also the deeper, often overlooked emotional and psychological causes. True vision extends beyond the confines of clear sight; it's about understanding oneself, confronting barriers, and experiencing the present wholly. The eyes, after all, are windows to the soul.

I believe that our eyes aren't just organs of sight but instruments of deeper understanding and connection. I see a world where the language of the eyes transcends words, revealing the **essence** of human spirit and potential. This is the future I envision, and with collective effort, I believe it's a vision we can make a reality.

In our modern world, artificial visual aids have become commonplace. A significant percentage of the population relies on these to navigate their daily lives. We are now witnessing the increasing dependence on glasses worldwide, with more than 90 percent of people over fifty wearing glasses. Yet it's startling to note that as a society, we often neglect the root causes of our deteriorating vision, both physical and metaphorical.

For me, this journey of self-discovery and eye rejuvenation started when I chose to challenge the status quo. Seventeen years with glasses was enough. Through commitment and the right mindset, I regained my vision, both for reading and distance, in a span of six months. This experience was not just about ditching the glasses; it opened doors to opportunities and perspectives I hadn't fathomed.

In delving more deeply into our vision issues, emotional and psychological roots often surface. Whether it's a traumatic event from the past or a fear of facing certain truths, confronting these barriers can pave the way to clarity. A key question I often ask people is "What is it you didn't want to see?"

The pinnacle of true vision is the ability to live in the present. It's about embracing each moment and seizing opportunities that come our way. As we align ourselves with this, our vision and perception of the world sharpen.

Eyesight isn't just about physical clarity. It's the bridge between our inner world and the vast universe outside. When we allow ourselves to love and be loved without reservations, our true potential unveils. Imagine a world where we communicate soul to soul, using the universal language of the eyes. This is the vision of the future I see.

Barry Auchettl, from Australia, is known as The Blockbuster. As an international keynote speaker, he has spoken in ten countries. He is founder of Light Body Alignment, chief vision officer of The Vision School, creator of Conversations: An Inspirational Game, multiple bestselling author, and principal player and producer in the movie *Vision 2020: From Eyesight to Insight*.

TheVisionSchool.org

FOR PETE'S SAKE

Pete Bartlett

I should be dead.

My story begins in Chappaqua, New York. I was adopted at just three months old. Born to a courageous mother who flew from Bermuda at eighteen to give birth in the New York Presbyterian Hospital, my early days were marked by potential and uncertainty.

Growing up with an older adopted brother who tormented me physically and emotionally with parents who were neglectful alcoholics, I started smoking marijuana in seventh grade.

My teenage years were a blur of drug and alcohol use, culminating with a stint in drug rehab at seventeen. After high school, I embraced a hedonistic lifestyle, indulging in substances ranging from marijuana to psychedelics. Moving to Telluride and later Steamboat Springs, Colorado, my life revolved around skiing and chasing highs.

The Grip of Addiction

Eventually I settled in Dickenson, North Dakota, where I received my first two driving while intoxicated (DWI) charges. While volunteering for Outward Bound in Leadville, Colorado, temporarily distracted me, my struggles with alcohol intensified.

Every day, I drank, and every night, I passed out. From magic mushrooms, ecstasy, and LSD to vodka, I was an adventurous user with only one aim: more.

My life felt out of control.

Hell, *I* was out of control, for Pete's sake!

From Leaves to Trees

A major turning point came in 1999 when I entered Alcoholics Anonymous (AA) and achieved ninety days of sobriety.

I was thirty-one years old and clean for the first time since seventh grade. I'd also found my calling—tree care.

Now, it might seem like a stretch to go from smoking pot to caring for trees, but volunteering for Outward Bound in Colorado had impacted me significantly. Among the trees, I learned about the bounty of nature. Surrounded by them, I felt peaceful.

I decided to get my commercial driver's license so I could operate heavy equipment, and I became certified through the International Society of Arborists as a tree care professional.

I loved my work. I loved my sobriety. For Pete's sake, my life was turning around!

For Pete's Sake

I Couldn't Stop Screaming

Then it happened.

One day, I was cutting out the top of a dead American Ash tree, sixty feet above the ground, when my chain saw "pinched."

Oh-oh!

Working with ash trees, especially dead ones, is always dangerous because the trees become very brittle. I saw the decayed heartwood as I made my pie cut (the one on the opposite side of the trunk). Carefully, I made the back cut.

Crack!

The tree splintered, and the branch twenty-five feet above me fell on top of me instead of away from me. Within seconds, it snapped both of my femurs. I couldn't move; I was tethered to the tree and totally helpless.

I passed out from the pain, and when I came to, a fellow arborist had climbed up and was lowering me down with him. Every time my legs bumped against the tree, I screamed!

From the tree to the ambulance to the helicopter that medevac'd me to Westchester County Medical Center, I couldn't stop screaming.

From Bad to Worse

The standard protocol at the time was for doctors to treat pain with opiates. So, the hospital prescribed

39

Oxycontin. Immediately, I was hooked. And for the next fifteen years, Oxycontin became my drug of choice, leading me from bad to worse.

In 2003, I received my third DWI charge and lost my license for a year, which propelled me back into AA. I got sober, and I was able to get my old job back after a year of sobriety. Boy, did it feel good to be among the trees again!

But the lure of drugs and alcohol was too strong, and in 2010, my life blew up when I received my fourth DWI.

Life Explodes

In one fell swoop, I lost my driver's license, my job, my apartment, and my will to live, all on the same day. In a desperate act to end my life, I downed a whole bottle of Klonopin, a sedative prescribed to treat panic attacks and anxiety.

When that didn't kill me, I ended up taking refuge at an emergency drop-in shelter in White Plains, New York. Four months later, I moved into a better homeless shelter where I met a drug dealer named Smiley and started mainlining heroin.

When I received news of my mother's passing, followed two weeks later by my dad's, it felt surreal to me. I was depressed, severely mentally ill—I had refused treatment for my bipolar II disorder—and numb to all emotions.

Heroin was my escape. Even during my father's memorial service, I shot up in the bathroom, oblivious to my world collapsing around me. I didn't care. And when I went to jail for my fourth DWI, I considered my life to be over.

Drinking had brought me to my knees, and heroin had blown up my life.

Call 911 or Die

In the wake of my parents' passing, I inherited a substantial sum—$500,000. Instead of using it for a fresh start, I used it to bounce from one rehab center to the next in California, splitting my inheritance between upscale long-term rehab facilities and my new drug of choice— methamphetamine (meth).

In 2012, I was living in an assisted living facility in Los Angeles, lying around smoking meth and drinking vodka, when I awoke one morning to throbbing pain in my right leg.

At that moment, I had a choice: Call 911 or die.

Amputee

On September 6, the ambulance took me to Cedars-Sinai Hospital in Los Angeles, where the attending physician met me with grave news: "Peter, you're experiencing deep vein thrombosis (DVT) in your right leg. There are five blood clots in your femoral artery, and we're taking you into surgery now."

After surgery, the doctor met with me and said: "Pete, we had to amputate the leg."

"What? You mean my leg is gone?"

"From the knee down, yes."

I later found out that it was a combination of lying around for so long without activity, smoking pot, and drinking vodka that caused the DVT. In addition, it triggered an autoimmune disease called Lupus Anticoagulant Syndrome that I'll have to live with for the rest of my life.

For the Love of Bub

After I was released from Cedar-Sinai, I went to a nursing home in Santa Monica, California, along with my stump and my demons. After I got out of there, I went to another rehabilitation facility in Riverside, California. There, I got ripped off by other residents, shot heroin, and met Bub.

Bub was a Blue Nose Pit Bull who belonged to Jack, a homeless junkie who, from time to time, would come by and ask me to watch his dog. I loved dogs, so I always said yes and was happy for the company.

"Hey man, can you watch my dog for three days?" he asked.

"Sure, I'd be happy to."

Three days turned into a week, and still Jack didn't return.

Meanwhile, I began investing in Bub. When Jack turned him over to my care, he was emaciated and infested with fleas. His fur was falling out, and patches of skin were showing from all his scratching.

I gave him a bath, put a flea collar on him, and started feeding him regularly. Bub quickly stopped itching and started filling out, and his one-year-old puppy energy emerged. I was in love!

So when Jack returned three weeks later demanding his dog, I said, "No."

Bub was mine, and I was his. With Bub, I'd found a reason to live, and by caring for Bub, I was caring about myself and positively moving forward.

Christmas with Bub

On Christmas Day 2015, Bub and I watched *It's a Wonderful Life* on the TV in a hotel room in Arcata, California. At the end of the movie, I turned to Bub and said, "I don't want to live like this anymore."

(Bub agreed.)

I quit heroin, moved back to New York, and started attending AA meetings. Then, in 2017, my friend Chip invited me to church, and Christ Church Episcopal Church in Tarrytown became my spiritual home.

After eight years, I got my driver's license back, and Bob, my former boss at Westchester Tree Life, rehired me to consult and troubleshoot tree care from the ground.

I faced my bipolar II diagnosis and the stigma surrounding it, started seeing a psychiatrist, and got my medication adjusted. Best yet, March 1, 2024, marks the one-year milestone of my sobriety.

What I Want You to Know

The reason I've shared my story is so you'll know these five things:

1. No matter how bad it gets, there's always hope.
2. If you're struggling with mental illness, get help.
3. Battling addiction is an ongoing journey. Never give up.
4. Find your spiritual path. Belief in something greater than yourself will help you through your darkest times.
5. Above all else, love yourself.

Let my story remind us that we all can rise above our challenges and navigate toward a brighter future—for Pete's sake and yours.

 **Pete Bartlett** lives with his dog and best friend, Bub, in New York, where he works as a tree consultant. While overcoming the challenges of addictions and mental illness, Pete inspires others to take control of their life, to love themselves, and to have faith during their darkest hours of need.

courageousimpact.com

FROM LEADING
AS A WAY OF
BEING TO BEING
AS A WAY OF LEADING

TiffanyNoelle Brown, PhD

"It's gonna be a great day, great day, great day, greaaaaat day!"
My seven-year-old and I are singing our made-up morning car ride song as we head back home from one of my kiddo's favorite places in the world—the library!

It was a great day! We had just gotten back a few days before from our O-fish-ally Adopted Trip to Disneyland. Life was good. My kiddo came into my life almost two years ago. I dreamt of her. I wrote a high school paper called *The Adoption Option*. I was adamant that I wanted to be a foster-adoptive parent. I screened potential life partners for their enthusiasm to go all in on that dream with me. Being a foster-adoptive mom was my destiny.

My dream came true. I am Mom. My kiddo's *Mommy.* A legally recognized mom. Forever.

After taking the time off "work" to become a mom, I missed my roles as executive director of Own Your Own Health, the nonprofit I founded and instructor, adjunct teaching Sociology and Medicine at the local university. I'm looking forward to being in those formal leadership positions again.

And . . . I'm excited to be more than *just* my kiddo's mom. (*Shhh!* My sense of self depends on it.) I want to continue applying my formal training and lead by empowering budding family and student leaders by making diversity, equity, inclusion, and belonging (DEI-B) concepts applicable, engaging, and empowering in the classroom and in the healthcare system.

> The light changes. Green: go. Following the green arrow at the T in the road, I turn left to go up the hill.
> I look to my left as I'm turning. I see a car stopped at the light in one lane, and I see another car coming down the hill toward the intersection. They have the red light. Stop! I have a green light. Go!
> I see the car coming through the intersection—right toward my door. Everything is in slow motion. Uh-oh! The car isn't stopping. I slam on my brakes. My

sunglasses fly off my face and land on the passenger-side floor. No airbag. No blood. I didn't hit my head. All good.

My kiddo! There was no cry, no scream, nothing. Silence. I look in the back seat to check on her. She is totally engrossed in her book. Of course she is. Everything is okay. It's just a car.

But that green arrow was leading me to a much different path than the one I anticipated. A day off from school became the day I became off, even more off than normal. Sure, I knew about concussions. But my eyes weren't dilated. I was just shaken up and tired from the adrenaline crash. So I took a nap.

I woke up with some neck pain and called my chiropractor who referred me to a chiropractor colleague who specialized in car accidents. For three years I went to the chiropractor, did physical therapy, eye therapy, and had multiple versions of special glasses all in an effort to deal with the whiplash and bulging discs detected in my neck and spine. But, once the physical issues were better, I was still having trouble.

Driving gave me migraines. I really had trouble with lights, sunlight or overhead lights. A half hour on my computer would knock out my energy for days. Even with my fancy-schmancy glasses, I still had trouble reading. It would be years before I would read an entire book again.

Finally my doctor suggested that I get a neurological test. Just to rule everything else out. Just so I would know.

"But, really," my doctor told me, "you are too high functioning to be impaired. You aren't disabled."

I'm not *disabled*. My issues are mostly invisible and explained away by others as "normal" forgetfulness. But it wasn't my normal forgetfulness. I used to remember names and details about people. I never missed an appointment. I was always on top of all the details of my work and timing of things.

I can never predict when the forgetfulness will show up, truly crippling me, or when I could cover for it, or when I was what appeared to be my "normal" self. I am too high functioning for others to notice when I am really struggling to pull up what I know, to find the right words, to not be too exhausted, to show up how I want to, how I remember I did.

I have been told by people who knew me before that I was "so high-functioning that my deficiency is still above most people's normal." When I choose to show up, that is. When I choose not to make myself invisible because my brain isn't working the way I remember it working.

But, when you look at the test results . . . I am a mere shell of myself, no matter how high functioning I appear to the outside world.

> "Severely impaired . . . below average . . . not able to teach anymore . . . high-functioning traumatic brain injury."

Because I was tested twenty-nine months after the accident, I missed the window of opportunity to heal the parts of my brain that were injured. I was told that if injuries occurred more than eighteen to twenty-four months after an injury, the brain damage is permanent.

I also was diagnosed with PTSD early on because of the impact I feared the accident had on my kiddo. Not the impact it had on me—or so I thought. The true PTSD later revealed itself in the loss of my former self, in my former navigation using the best maps to take the "best" route to get to my destinations. I had to constantly renavigate the world and my place in it.

Although I elevated the voices of many categories of "disabled" populations and recognized and highlighted their abilities in my work before the accident, I could not see those qualities in myself. People would tell me:

> "It's just something you have to accept."
> "Everyone forgets things."
> "I would never have noticed."

But I notice. I notice if I am impaired. I am assessing myself for "readiness" minute-to-minute.

And the same advice keeps coming my way from a few great coaches, mentors, and friends:

> "You would never be this hard on someone else living with the same situation. What would you tell that person?"

I would help them see what they are still and newly capable of now that they weren't before. I would advocate for them; I would empower them to advocate for themselves whenever possible. And I would be patient. I would listen. I would invite them to show up just as they are.

It's always hard to take our own advice, isn't it? But being gently reminded of this over and over . . . because I forgot . . . or maybe I just didn't believe in myself at that moment . . . this guidance is just what I needed and continue to need every day.

My doctors told me not to tell people that I have a Traumatic Brain Injury because I would never get another job. My coach Deb King was the first mentor to allow me to be myself in my new state. I don't have to lead or work in a specific way to be successful or impactful. The Wisdom Playground was the first place I was embraced for showing up—for just being me and being there, I was not only valued, but valuable.

Deb encouraged me to gain entry into my inclusion work by sharing about my TBI because it exemplifies my life's work in diversity, equity, inclusion, and belonging, trauma, well-being, and empowerment without the prickliness and polarization that typically comes from work in "inclusion."

Finally feeling safe enough to show up as I am, just being who I am now, sharing about my TBI, I have found a new way to empower shifts in perspectives. Living with a TBI is a new opening, a new route, to articulate the impact of being marginalized and silenced through no fault of my own, but by circumstances—which has been my message about the value of marginalized and silenced people all along.

By just being, I am leading, as a role model to my kiddo and others with invisible and visible "disabilities." I am leading by doing business differently. I am leading by showing up as I am, how I am, in the moment. By recognizing and utilizing my cap-ABILITIES. By sharing my wisdom, both formal and through lived experiences. By expressing my passion from a different perspective, I am allowing myself to belong, as I am. I am leading by being.

And by virtue of you having chosen this book at this moment, I know that you are seeking to lead in some way in your own life. Bringing your experiences along with you is important. I am living proof that being itself is also leading.

Dr. TiffanyNoelle Brown, PhD, is a world-renowned interactive speaker and trainer, bestselling author, and founder of Nurturing Youth Leaders. Her work focuses on expanding the application of what it means to be a leader based on six key areas: cape-ABILITIES, wisdom, well-being, passions, belonging, and leadership.

TiffanyNoelleBrown.com

DISCOVERING TRUE BEAUTY

Jennifer Butler

Anu worked for eight and a half years at the same job without a raise or promotion. In the following eighteen months, she earned five promotions and five raises.

Michele's real estate career skyrocketed—moving from an average producer to the top 1 percent of her profession.

After thirty years of marriage, Kim's husband looked up from his desk and said, "Wow!"

After several rounds of chemo and losing all her hair, Afton chose not to wear wigs—she just wore her colors, and everyone around her told her she looked beautiful.

What do these women have in common?

They learned how to tap into the secret power of color!

Studies show that 93 percent of communication is nonverbal. That means that how we show up in the world is more important than we sometimes realize. Note: The hiring executive at Anu's company said she had the job when she got off the elevator. What was different? The color and silhouette of her clothing!

My first exposure to the psychology of color harmonies was in the fashion industry in 1979. While working at Bloomingdale's in New York, I was asked to dress Joan Holmes, the president of The Hunger Project, for a special symposium that was bringing together all the major charities uniting to end world hunger. She wanted clothing to empower the mission.

When we met, Joan showed me colors chosen specifically to suit her. It was an epiphany for me—the colors were her! Another surprise was the color we chose for her in her role as moderator. Instead of the expected navy, black or gray, we found her skin tone—a color that fosters fellowship and trust. The response from the audience was immediate; wearing her color of intimacy set the tone for what became a very successful event.

The experience rocked my world. I had loved color since I was a little girl in my mother's fabric store, but seeing color used in this way to communicate a specific feeling and empower a personal mission—especially a vision as significant as wiping out world hunger—was a new experience.

Many of us wear colors that we are attracted to, which are not necessarily the colors that make us more attractive. Pictures of me from different times in my life reveal many beautiful outfits, but they were not really "me." I, like many other women, shopped trends, styles, and colors I liked. But I ended up with a closet full of clothes and nothing to wear. Clearly, there was something else important for me to learn.

When I met Suzanne Caygill, the originator of Color Harmony Theory, and learned to paint my own coloring, I began to understand the true value of color. By painting the pigments that create the colors of my hair, skin, and eyes, I was able to see the sacred relationship of those three interdependent colors. With that knowledge, I was able to be authentic in my clothing choices.

Originally, I believed my skin has a pink base, like my mother's. In fact, it is peach. My warm brown eyes are really amber. And my hair, now silver, was a dark warm brown.

It's interesting how we create a projection of ourselves. When we dress that projection, we are lost in translation.

Meeting and studying with Suzanne was a pivotal moment in my life and career. Now my closet is full of clothes where everything works. The colors are harmonious. The styles flatter my body. I adopt the trends that work for me and ignore those that don't. I am able to successfully combine purchases from decades ago with new items to create fantastic outfits that seem brand-new and timeless.

Most importantly, I honor myself from the inside out and from the outside in.

It's important for me to tell this story because so many women have given up on personal style. They live in a state of resignation, triggered by social media, fast fashion, and pursuit of nonexistent idealized perfection.

Everything Suzanne taught me inspires me to empower my own clients. I'm committed to shifting our way of living from image to essence. The truth is that each of us is born with a unique color harmony and style blueprint that perfectly honors us. Following that harmony and sacred design creates true beauty.

Our culture encourages us to look outward for a definition of beauty. In reality, all of the keys to beauty are *within us*.

Let me share with you what a color palette really is: It is the harmonic convergence of energy in physical form that creates you as a human being.

Each aspect of your own coloring has a special meaning. Your natural hair color creates the foundation for your life—it is used for all your basics: shoes, handbags, hats, coats, dresses, slacks, tops, and accessories.

How, you ask, does someone buy accessories in their hair color? Brown hair necessitates bronze or copper jewelry. Blonde hair looks best in gold or antique brass. Silver hair wears antique silver or pewter. These are just a few examples. Jewelry can also come from other colors in your palette. More about those colors to come.

The next important color is your natural skin tone (not spray-tanned or with heavy makeup). Your skin tone facilitates intimacy, friendship, and self-love. It's the basis for your makeup foundation and blush tone. Skin tone is often used for painting family rooms or bedrooms.

The final color in the sacred triad is your eye color. It's important to look at the lights of your eyes. Brown eyes may be amber, copper, cinnamon, or gold. Hazel eyes might be pine needle green, sage, or olive. Wearing these colors creates a sense of balance and equilibrium.

Everyone has their own shade of red, an extension of their skin tone. Your red might be pink, coral, orange, rust, garnet, carnelian, burgundy, or any number of other "red" hues. Worn in the shade the works for you, your red (or orange, or pink, etc.) inspires passion and celebration.

An extended color palette includes accent colors that create drama and command attention. These are colors that support us or express support for others. The palette also includes examples of the types of prints, sizes, and scale that most honor your individual design. And it offers an array of metallics that will inform your choices in jewelry, clothing, and home accessories such as lamps and other fixtures.

In forty years of working with more than seven thousand individual clients to help them fully and authentically express themselves using color and style, the recurring "aha" is recognizing the importance of knowing their "inner light." Suzanne Caygill recognized that humanity falls into four seasons, which represent the cycle of life.

- Springs give joy and emanate the sunlight.
- Summers provide grace and emanate twilight.
- Autumns reap the abundant harvest and emanate firelight.
- Winters strive for mastery and show discernment. They emanate the moonlight.

Recognizing your archetype is the key to expressing your authenticity.

The key to the Spring personality can be expressed in three words: Renew, Rejuvenate, and Rejoice. We call the Spring man the rogue or the rascal and the Spring woman the coquette. Springs have the gift of being instantly relatable, and they bring in fresh ideas and inspiration. We call them our "cheerleaders" because they have the ability to cheer us up and to cheer us on. They inspire us through laughter, by not taking life too seriously, and through their ability to simplify and give a new perspective.

Summers are sustaining and nurturing. The Summer woman is the princess or the lady. The Summer man is the gentleman or the gentle man. Summers are thoughtful in nature with a keen sense of refinement. They tend to see life's subtle intricacies, and thus do not make instant decisions or give simple answers. They have an innate sense of order, a sense of timeliness and appropriateness. They are subtle.

Autumns are intensely independent and excel at producing results. We call the Autumn man the rugged man and the Autumn woman the lioness. Autumns are generous, and able to create abundance. They are also known for their strong wills and straightforward communication. As Suzanne Caygill once said, "[Autumns] would rather be fervently wrong than tepidly right." They remind us to stay grounded and focused. They are centered and dynamic individuals.

Winters are a study in contrast—they possess dramatic and intense personalities and exude sophistication and self-containment. We call the Winter woman the priestess or the moon goddess and the Winter man the hero or the man of the hour. Winters have the gift of discernment. They value mastery. Because they live in extremes, Winters are abstract thinkers who are excellent at providing clear-cut answers. Winters love culture and the arts and often do best in an urban environment surrounded by the best of civilization.

I am immensely grateful to all the women and men who have joined the True Beauty Movement. They choose to live fully expressed, sharing who they are from the inside out. It takes courage to be seen. And it's even more inspiring when we leverage our full self-expression to accomplish our larger mission on earth.

Jennifer Butler is the leading expert in the sociology of style and color. She develops style and color palettes that reveal the essence of an individual's personality and allow them to powerfully, authentically, and effectively express themselves. Her clients range from CEOs and business executives to celebrities, artists, and community leaders.

JenniferButlerColor.com

BEING
ON
PURPOSE

Elaine Chung

Everyone is talking about purpose these days!

From self-help gurus to motivational speakers, the quest for one's life purpose has become a ubiquitous topic of discussion. It's as if we're all on a grand cosmic scavenger hunt, desperately searching for that elusive golden ticket that will grant us access to a life of eternal fulfillment and meaning.

Doesn't this sound exhausting?

The idea that we have a preordained, singular purpose waiting to be discovered is questionable. Are we really to believe that the universe has assigned us all something specific to be?

Considering the sheer diversity of human experience, I find it hard to believe that a person's purpose is one thing for all their life. And don't get me started on what the pressure of finding your life's purpose can do to you!

People often feel guilty or inadequate if they haven't uncovered their "true calling" by a certain age or if their interests don't neatly align with what society deems purposeful. This societal obsession with purpose can inadvertently rob us of the simple joys of life—the moments of spontaneity, exploration, and personal growth that don't fit neatly into the grand narrative of a single life purpose.

Perhaps the reason lies in our desperate need for certainty and structure in an inherently uncertain and chaotic world. We hold on to the concept of a singular purpose to anchor ourselves in the face of life's unpredictability. But in doing so, we miss out on the beauty of embracing the unknown, of allowing ourselves the freedom to pivot, experiment, and redefine our paths as we discover new passions and interests.

Fluid Journey

Instead of treating purpose as a rigid destination, we could consider it a fluid journey—a journey filled with a series of experiences, relationships, and discoveries that shape us over time.

Maybe our purpose is not a fixed point on the horizon but rather a constellation of moments illuminating our lives in unexpected and meaningful ways.

Perhaps, in searching for our purpose, we realize our underlying yearning for something more profound:

- A connection to something larger than ourselves

- A sense of belonging
- A desire to leave a positive impact

Instead of getting caught up in the pressure to find the "one true purpose," perhaps we can find it in the very act of living—in our relationships, our growth, and our ability to make a difference, no matter how small or seemingly insignificant.

Ugh Bugs

I don't like bugs. Big bugs, little bugs, crawly bugs, flying bugs—they're all ugh bugs to me.

As you can imagine, I don't spend much time sitting in nature. But I do like being out in it. It's so lovely to get out of the city, feel the expanse of the sky above, breathe in the fresh air, and walk among the majestic trees looking for wildflowers.

One day, as part of a neuro-linguistic programming (NLP) class I was taking, we took a field trip to sit in silence among the trees.

Sit. Oh boy.

The purpose was to encourage us to venture into nature and attentively absorb the wisdom conveyed by the majestic trees and the natural world. And while there, to contemplate a question close to our hearts, then voice that question to the trees.

I chose a spot near an old, unused stone barbeque pit encircled by large rocks. It was a peaceful, soulful place.

There, I asked: "What is my purpose?"

That question wasn't hard for me to come up with since it was the same question that had haunted my thoughts for most of my life.

I yearned to know my purpose.

No Booming Voice

Gazing skyward, surrounded by the towering trees and the rustling leaves, I asked with a sincere and open heart and waited in hopeful anticipation for a booming voice to answer: "Elaine, your purpose is . . ."

All I heard were the nearby crickets. So, I asked again: "What is my purpose?"

Time trickled on as I remained seated amid the rocks, trees, and, yes, bugs. I shifted uncomfortably, my fidgety feet working to evade the creeping insects from crawling on my legs.

I asked again.

The anticipation dwindled as minutes stretched to an hour. No booming voice shattered the silence, and the grand revelation I yearned for never materialized.

I was so over this exercise!

With an inward sigh, I glanced at the ground and was alarmed to see an army of ants trekking back and forth in front of me!

More curious than anything else, I leaned closer and focused on what the ants were doing.

Quietly Purposeful

Ants are amazing.

They go about their day with a unified purpose—collaboratively working within their colonies to find food, nurture and care for one another, and defend their home from predators.

Back and forth, I watched them go—quietly, purposeful.

Then, it hit me like a proverbial "ton of bricks": All this time, I'd been listening for a booming voice, when the ants were quietly there, showing me the answer.

You know how it's said that "when the student is ready, the teacher will appear"?[1]

Well, these ants were my teacher. Their ceaseless activity—carrying fragments to their colony, foraging for sustenance—resonated deeply. The message was clear: These creatures operated purposefully, needing no explicit command or revelation of their

---

1   Stephen Mitchel, *Tao Te Ching: A New English Version* (New York: Harper Collins, 2006), 54.

mission. They were living their purpose with an innate understanding of what it was.

The Way of Purpose

Is this the same for humans?

Do we wander about, immersed in our daily routines, and unknowingly serve a purpose? Is this what I had been listening for the booming voice to tell me?

I laughed out loud.

Like the ants, we don't need to know our purpose to fulfill it.

A smile shared, a kind word spoken—seemingly simple gestures that might ripple into profound effects on others. This is the way purpose works. The connections we foster, and the impact we make, could very well constitute the intricate threads of our purpose.

At that moment, among the rocks, trees, and, yes, even the bugs, I understood that while our human complexities might obscure our purpose's clarity, our existence has an inherent significance.

Is the way of purpose simply to be?

If yes, then being purposeful was the key.

Being on Purpose

In my book *Start Chasing Nothing*, I talk about how fleeting happiness is when we look outside ourselves for someone or something to make our life meaningful.

And it's the same with purpose. When we stop chasing after our purpose, trying to figure out what it is or should be, we begin to understand that our very being is our purpose.

Being on purpose is our purpose.

It's the Little Things

One day I ran into Lisa at a work-related gathering. She was a colleague of mine; however, she was from a different department, and we didn't regularly interact. So, I was surprised when she came up to me and said: "Elaine, I'm so glad you're here. I've been meaning to talk with you about something."

"Okay. What is it?"

"You always seem so confident when you present in meetings. I'm not."

Lisa explained that no matter how well prepared she was, she always got nervous, stumbled over her words, and, when asked questions, couldn't think straight.

"What can I do?" she implored.

"Lisa, the next time you're giving a presentation, how about we arrange a time for you to come to my office? That way, you can run through your presentation in front of me, and, if you'd like, I'll give you feedback."

"Yes! That would be great, Elaine. Thank you."

A Cookie of Appreciation

It was a small gesture of help. And I forgot about it over time when Lisa didn't take me up on it.

Until one day, Lisa showed up at my office bearing a small cookie—in Asian cultures, giving a cookie, cake, or other small treat is customary when someone resigns and leaves a company.

"Elaine, thank you for offering to help me with my presentation. Until then, I didn't think anyone cared about me at work."

Oh my, I thought to myself.

"You have no idea how much that brightened my day and filled me with hope."

Well, she was right about that. I had no idea!

Essence of Purpose

I was touched by what Lisa said. Not because I felt proud of what I did or valued by her appreciation. Instead, I felt humbled.

At that moment, perhaps for the first time, I understood that this is the essence of purpose. The realization that our purpose isn't something to be sought after but an ongoing narrative woven into our everyday existence.

Being on purpose is our purpose.

 **Elaine Chung** is the bestselling author of *Start Chasing Nothing* and co-author of *You Lead You*. An award-winning speaker, she presents workshops on personal and leadership development. Her uplifting message of hope and positivity helps individuals and groups lead themselves with inner conviction and outward confidence.

StartChasingNothing.com

HOW INTUITION SAVED MY EYE

Nanci Deutsch

On September 12, 2001, a day after the whole world witnessed the tragic collapse of the World Trade Center in New York City, I found myself navigating the familiar Seaford-Oyster Bay Expressway. People all over Long Island were in shock from all that was happening and not paying attention to things as they usually would.

Behind the wheel of my white Toyota Camry, I was returning home to Long Beach from a routine chiropractic visit. As the radio played, resonating with the hum of the road beneath my wheels, the melodic strains of "With Arms Wide Open" by Creed enveloped the car just as I neared a familiar stop sign. The poignant words of lead singer Scott Stapp hung in the air. Suddenly, my tranquility shattered as a big black Suburban slammed into the rear of my car.

Bam!

The left side of my head hit the steering wheel. Damage done—blood streamed down my face.

Not the First Time

As I waited for the ambulance to arrive, the haunting echoes of my past brushed against the present as I found myself in yet another car accident.

Six years prior, as I hurriedly crossed the street, a car crashed into me. My body flew up in the air and slammed into the windshield, my head cracking its surface. As I slid down the windshield onto the hood of the car, I thought: *Oh-oh. This could be it.*

While onlookers gaped in shock, I heard Spirit say, "No, it's not your time."

Miraculously, I didn't have a concussion, and no bones were broken. But I did have herniated discs in my neck and lower back. August 29, 1995, was my first near-fatal car accident and the first time I was aware that Spirit had intervened on my behalf.

Six years later, as the paramedics pulled me out of my Camry and strapped me to the gurney, I wondered again, *Could this be it?* And heard Spirit say, "No."

Upon arrival, the emergency room physician assessed the bleeding and, because of my facial injury, told the nurse to telephone the on-call plastic surgeon and have him come to the hospital.

As the plastic surgeon sutured the skin right above my eyebrow, unbeknownst to me, the true gravity of the situation was unfolding. An ordeal far beyond the initial impact awaited me.

Uncertain Prognosis

Even after the sutures were removed, I still had trouble seeing. There was swelling under my left eye and black-and-blue bruising around it. My vision was blurry, and I had almost no peripheral vision. The surgeon ordered an MRI to figure out what was going on.

When I next saw him, he said, "Nanci, upon careful examination of the MRI, it is evident that you've sustained an orbital floor fracture."

"A what?"

"An orbital floor fracture means that the orbital rim of your eye is pushing the bones back, causing the muscles and bones of the eye socket floor to buckle downward."

Oh my!

"You have two options: let it heal and see if your vision returns or surgery."

Surgery? I don't want to have surgery!

"Doctor, what happens if I don't have surgery?"

"Well, it's possible that your eye would recede into your eye socket, leaving your face disfigured and blind in that eye. However, you don't have to have the surgery. It could heal on its own."

Intuitive Knowing

I was thirty-nine. The last thing I wanted was surgery. Plus, I knew my body could heal if given enough time.

However, as soon as the surgeon told me what could happen if I didn't have surgery, I intuitively knew what my decision needed to be.

But I hadn't yet learned to trust my intuition. So, I made some phone calls to family and friends, seeking their opinions on what course of action to take. In reality, though, it was to validate and confirm what, deep down, I already understood what needed to be done.

Later that week, I called the surgeon and said, "Schedule me for surgery."

Three Weeks Later

On October 4, 2001, three weeks after the black Suburban crashed into my white Camry, I had surgery. The surgeon put in a titanium plate to protect my eye socket and stop the muscles from slipping into the gap caused by the fracture.

The next time I saw the surgeon, he said, "Nanci, it's a good thing you elected to have surgery. The damage was more extensive than we anticipated. Without surgery, your eye definitely would have receded, and you'd have gone blind in that eye."

From his perspective, my eye had narrowly escaped irreparable harm.

From my perspective, I intuitively knew the extent of the damage and what needed to be done.

The date of my surgery marked not only the physical reconstruction of my eye but was the turning point when I learned to trust my intuition in new and profound ways.

Everything Happens for a Reason

People often say, "Everything happens for a reason," when nothing else makes sense, and they don't know what else to say.

In my case, I grappled with the improbable outcomes of two separate car accidents—one that should have maimed me and another that would have robbed me of sight. And both could have killed me.

As I mulled this over, the only conclusion I could draw was that these two accidents happened so I could know without reservation that I was—and am—divinely protected and guided by Spirit. When I came to that realization, I knew it was time for me to shift into a new level of trust.

Second Chapter

To say that my life changed because of these two accidents would be an oversimplification of what occurred. My car accidents were exactly the catalysts I needed that prompted me to go inward and reevaluate my connection with intuition and Spirit.

The result?

A shift from not fully trusting my intuition to trusting it implicitly. From turning to external sources for validation and confirmation to tuning into my intuition for guidance and direction. This shift, more influential than the accidents themselves, is what redirected the trajectory of my life.

From a young age, I'd always known I would do something to positively impact many people and make a difference in the world, even though the *how* and *what* were unknown. And despite an inherent fear of public speaking, I envisioned addressing large audiences.

Before my eye surgery, I was talking to my friend Scott about what I was now calling my "second chapter" and how I was trusting my intuition to guide me where to next when he interjected: "Nanci, a good friend of mine is a local radio station manager. If you want to make a big impact, radio is a good place to start."

Radio? I've never thought of that!

"Yes," my intuition signaled.

"Okay!" I beamed at Scott.

The next thing I knew, I was doing a show called *Healing and Inspiration* on WGBB in New York that grew into what I do now. Today, I host and produce a weekly TV and radio talk show called *Inspired and Empowered Living* on W4WN.com that's podcasted on iHeart Radio to over one million listeners.

Deliberate Impacts

Looking back, I know that Spirit has been with me, guiding me on my path. I know that intuition saved my eye and that the car accidents weren't accidents—they were deliberate impacts. I now understand that:

- They were intended to impact my life.
- They impacted me so that I would move forward on my journey.
- They were necessary for me to impact the world with my message.

From these deliberate impacts, in addition to being a Licensed Clinical Social Worker (LCSW) for more than thirty years, I've become a certified hypnotherapist and intuitive coach. I started my business in 2005, and ten years later I developed the

Intuition Advantage System, a step-by-step process that helps others feel more confident when making intuitive-based decisions.

Intuitive-Based Decision-Making

When making decisions, it isn't just about following your intuition. While that's the most essential part, it isn't the only one. Here are three key elements that will help you make intuitive-based decisions:

1. **Center yourself:** As you venture into any decision, take a moment to center yourself before tuning into your intuition.
2. **Tap into greater knowing:** It's important to connect to something greater than yourself such as God, Spirit, the Divine, universe, or angels.
3. **Embrace present awareness:** Stay open and be receptive to the information unfolding in the present moment. In intuitive-based decision-making, striking a balance between the head and the heart is key. You know you're in alignment when feeling the emotions of peace, love, joy, and gratitude. Then you know your decisions are coming from your highest self.

Trust your intuition; it always knows what's best for you.

With more than thirty years of experience, **Nanci Deutsch, LCSW, CHt**, guides individuals to their best selves. She has developed The Intuition Advantage System and hosts the *Inspired and Empowered Living* TV show. Nanci uniquely combines her counseling, coaching, and intuitive abilities to transform lives through training programs, groups, and individual work.

NanciDeutsch.com

WALKING
ON
WATER
Christy Modita Engels

Life often throws me curves that seem to get in the way of my plans. Later, I discover that those curves were leading to something good. This is such a story.

Even as a child, I expected to have a lifelong career as an elementary school teacher. However, life threw me a curve, and I ended up teaching for only about eight years. I quit when I was thirty because I was burned out and exasperated with the way the school district treated the children. I taught at a school where the children were poor and brown-skinned, and which lacked supplies and services. Eventually the district sent a representative to tell our staff to stop making requests for psychological services, stating that all the children's problems were due to their environment. This made me feel helpless.

Once I quit, things began falling together, but I didn't know for what purpose. I took a career planning class. My top three job priorities were that I would be able use the bathroom when I needed to, I would have a lunch break, and I would not have a bunch of people in my face while I was working. I chose to take a five-month course to become a paralegal. I didn't feel any vocation for the law, but the job fit my three priorities, and the course wouldn't take long.

When I interviewed for jobs, I didn't like the private law firms I visited. The attorneys were rude, and paralegals were not treated well. Then I went for an interview with a legal aid office. The attorneys were crazy in a good way. I liked them. They hired me for two unexpected reasons. They were just starting to represent children under the Education of All Handicapped Act and were looking for someone like me who could read school records. I also had the skills to organize the huge pile of documents that were sitting around in their office. Interesting curves that led me to a paralegal job related to education.

I ended up representing children with special needs at informal hearings. Paralegals can represent clients at such hearings, but not in the court. I worked with a supervising attorney who specialized in education, and we developed trainings for other staff. I loved this work, and it provided some vindication for the way the district had behaved. It was a great job. Again, it was nothing I could have imagined when I planned my career as a teacher.

At first, I had no interest in being an attorney. Then I began to be unhappy about the way the attorneys handled my cases on appeal. Another curve. Finally, I decided to apply to law school at the age of thirty-five. This also was not in my childhood picture of my career.

I began law school in 1981. At the time, it was still unusual for women to go to law school and become lawyers. Plus, I had issues I needed to deal with before I could make the commitment. I felt like I was too old, and I had concerns about being a woman attorney. I worked on these until I was ready to apply to law school. I attended law school at night, and during the day, I had a private practice representing children with special needs at hearings. I enjoyed it.

I began practicing law when I was forty-one. I worked various places, including doing tort litigation and personal injury. When I began my own practice, I expected to handle special education cases. Then the supervising attorney from legal aid threw me a curve. She had opened her own private practice representing children with special needs. She was concerned that if I started a similar practice, it would dilute the work. Instead, she asked me to refer to her the special education cases and she would refer to me any related issues having to do with an injury to the child. I agreed, not knowing where this might lead.

In those days, it was still rare for a woman to be an attorney. Very often, male attorneys played hardball with each other at every stage of the case. Because I was a woman, they assumed that they had an upper hand with me. My approach to this was to be polite and accommodating until it became necessary to be otherwise. This made these attorneys think I was a pushover until they found out differently.

One of the cases I handled had to do with a little girl who broke her arm in school. This little girl had a mental disability that would keep her from ever learning anything beyond preschool skills. She was on a jungle gym and fell off, and it appeared that there hadn't been any staff nearby keeping an eye on her. Her mother came to me because she felt this should not have happened to her daughter. She was also very upset because, due to her daughter's disability, her daughter could not understand what had happened to her, what the doctors were doing, or why she had to wear a cast. Her mother felt the school should have prevented this accident.

The first step in a lawsuit is to file the Complaint. The Complaint lists all the facts of the case and what the Plaintiff contends. We filed the Complaint and alleged that there was insufficient supervision and that the damages were due to that insufficient supervision. We sought monetary damages and guarantees of better supervision.

Once the Complaint has been filed, the Defendant, in this case the school district, responds to the Complaint by filing an Answer. In the Answer, the school district contended that none of the damages were caused by insufficient supervision.

We then entered the Discovery phase of litigation. In Discovery, each side exchanges written questions, called Interrogatories. I sent Interrogatories to the school district, including something called Form Interrogatories, which are written and approved of by the court.

If the defense doesn't like any of the Interrogatories, they can file a motion asking that those questions be thrown out. Before they file the motion, the defense counsel must meet with plaintiff's counsel, discuss their objections to the interrogatories, and resolve any issues. Since the Form Interrogatories are already approved by the court, the defense cannot object to those.

In a major curve, the attorney for the school district objected to the Form Interrogatories. I politely wrote to him explaining that Form Interrogatories cannot be objected to and gave him all the laws supporting that position. He refused to accept that. At this point, I began to be less accommodating and polite. I met with him and explained again why he had to answer the Form Interrogatories. He disagreed and filed a motion with the court.

Once he filed his motion, I filed an Opposition. I included the same arguments. I asked that money sanctions be paid to me to make up for all the time and energy spent arguing this unnecessary issue. I won on the motion, and the attorney paid me the money sanctions with his own personal check. From that time on, he changed his whole approach to the case and acted powerless. Because he had so many assumptions about me as a woman attorney, he seemed incapable of understanding that what I had argued wasn't some kind of magic; it was just solid law.

At the end of the case before the trial, we had a Settlement Conference with the judge. Each attorney met separately with the judge in his chambers. The judge met with the opposing attorney first. When I met with the judge, he told me he didn't think we had any case. He then went on to say that the opposing attorney was, for some reason, willing to settle. He added that he and the opposing attorney had gone to law school together, and that the opposing attorney was a jerk then as well. He stated he would not dissuade the attorney from settling.

When we all returned to the courtroom, each attorney sat next to their client facing the judge's podium. The judge read the settlement granting my client sixty thousand dollars for her daughter. While he was doing so, he turned toward my client's mother and said to her, "I think it's a case with no liability, and if it were tried in front of me, I would make the ruling that you wouldn't get anything. I think that your attorney has done a remarkable job for you. I think that you should consider that *she walks on water.*"

I ordered the transcript of that statement, and I still have it. I referred my client to a probate attorney who could help her set up a special needs trust for her daughter. I was really glad that my strategy had worked, and that life had supplied all the curves that led to this moment.

Food for thought:

1. What curves have you encountered thus far in your life?
2. How have those curves led to outcomes you never expected?

 **Christy Modita Engels** is a retired attorney and educator. She is a teller of inspirational stories, a singer of sacred songs, and a visual artist. She has a diverse background as a storyteller, singer, dancer, writer, educator, artist, musician, minister, attorney, and mediator.

instagram.com/@christymoditacreations

UNBROKEN DREAMS

CaS Facciponti

Rumi once wrote, "The wound is the place where the Light enters you." On May 28th, 1996, I discovered the profound truth in these words as I embarked on a journey into the depths of my own courage and resilience.

The sun shone brilliantly on the winding roads of Staten Island, New York. Six of us had squeezed into a two-door Ford Escort and were driving through a forest with towering trees whose branches intertwined like ancient guardians. I, a young girl, felt a mix of exhilaration and trepidation in the front seat. As we approached the dense woods, time itself seemed to hold its breath. My senses sharpened, and a profound shroud of terror descended. I somehow knew we were on the precipice of calamity. The air resonated with the crescendo of my companions' screams, their voices a tumultuous cascade of panic.

The impending collision arrived like an apocalyptic symphony, a deafening crescendo of shattering glass and splintering dreams. Upon impact with the trees, I went unconscious. It was the kind of nothingness that felt like an eternity, a black void without awareness. What jolted me back to reality was the frantic commotion in the back seat. I was disoriented, but I could hear the muffled voices and feel the shuffling movements behind me. The four people in the back seat were climbing out the passenger door, pushing my seat forward in their rush, my semiconscious body still in it. Their hasty escape unknowingly worsened my injuries, causing further organ damage.

I opened my eyes to the horror of the aftermath. My sister's mangled hand, a sacrifice to save herself from the windshield, bore silent testament to the violence of the collision. Her brand-new purple letter jacket, once a symbol of achievement, was now drenched in blood from her head wound, and her face was unrecognizable from the impact.

As days turned to weeks, the hospital room became my world—a space where the pangs of agony harmonized with the strains of hope. Machines and tubes became my loyal attendants, guardians of my every heartbeat and breath. Days bled into nights, the sterile ceiling an ever-present witness to my struggle.

Pain, an unrelenting tempest, swept through my body, gnawing at my very core. My back was fractured, my future an enigma. Yet within me, an inferno of determination raged. I clung to the message of a movie I watched nearly every day I was hospitalized, *Rudy*. It was the tale of a young man who had defied the odds to play football at Notre Dame. His story became a beacon and then a lodestar for my journey.

Rudy's indomitable spirit became my compass in the abyss of despair. I contemplated how he had never yielded to the shadows that loomed over his dreams, and that same spirit ignited within me. I was resolute; I would not allow the accident to inscribe the narrative of my life.

The weeks transitioned into months, and with the unwavering guidance of doctors and nurses, I embarked on the labyrinthine path of physical therapy. Each step I took became an overture of resilience; each stretch was a masterpiece of triumph. The spirit of Rudy and my untiring willpower propelled me forward, driving me to rise from the wreckage of my former self, one painstaking step at a time.

As my recovery blossomed, I understood the significance of the college application process. My aspirations could not be tethered to the confines of a hospital room; they soared, carried by the winds of possibility. My determination anchored my belief in the power of academic and athletic scholarships to shape my future. I toiled ceaselessly, each assignment a canvas where I painted my heart's desires, every workout an opus of dedication. My earlier experience in track and field had been abridged by the accident, but I refused to concede my dreams. Instead, I embraced a new sport, racewalking, an endeavor approved by my physicians.

Racewalking was a ballet of endurance, a performance where every step was a brushstroke of precision and every breath laden with determination. In this sport, one's connection with the ground was an unbroken kiss, where the leg remained rigid from the instant of impact with the ground until reaching the vertical position. Each stride was a dance, a marriage of technique, focus, and intensity. I invested countless hours refining my form, mastering the nuances of the sport. Racewalking tested the limits of my dedication, yet with every step, I inched closer to my dreams.

My swiftest mile in racewalking was a mesmerizing 6:42, where time itself seemed to halt in awe. The fastest two miles I raced was 14:04, a duet of moments that wove together an anthem of unwavering determination. These accomplishments transcended mere statistics; they were a testimony to my persistence and an ode to the tenacity that had buoyed me through the darkest shadows of despair.

The media took note, weaving tales of my journey and celebrating victories in local and regional competitions. My story was one of resilience, a testament to human potential, and a glimpse into a sport rarely understood. Racewalking, I found, was more than a sport; it was my sanctuary and my crucible. It mirrored my own journey of perseverance, where precision and determination were my closest companions. Just as I had redefined myself after the accident, I now reshaped my physical limitations.

The story, however, did not culminate with my recovery or my achievements in racewalking. My journey at West Point was an extraordinary odyssey. I ascended through the ranks, surmounting each challenge with the same unyielding determination that had borne me through the darkest hours. My scholastic prowess had secured my place among the top ten cadets in my class, yet it was my leadership qualities that set me apart. I became a beacon to my peers, exemplifying the essence of a leader in every endeavor. In a corps of cadets numbering 4,400, divided into four regiments, each with a cadet commander and approximately 1,100 cadets, the honor of being appointed as Regimental Commander was a reverberating crescendo of my commitment and dedication. The position was imbued with responsibility and honor, and I accepted it with grace and humility.

On a crisp, starry evening, an occasion was adorned with grandeur and significance. One of many West Point banquets, an illustrious gathering of cadets, distinguished guests, and alumni had descended upon the hallowed halls of the institution.

The mess hall, resplendent with shimmering decor and meticulously set tables, was a tapestry of elegance, where history and tradition melded seamlessly.

Amidst this opulent backdrop, I found myself at the pinnacle of my cadet journey. The event was an embodiment of the Academy's ethos, a celebration of leadership, scholarship, and the indomitable human spirit. It was an evening where stories of courage and accomplishment wove together to inspire, and I was about to share my own chapter with a luminary audience.

As I stood before the distinguished delegate at that momentous banquet, my thoughts journeyed through the expanse of my life. I had traversed a treacherous path from the wreckage of a car accident to the revered halls of West Point. This journey had been one of courage, perseverance, and unbroken dreams.

During that special evening, a distinguished delegate leaned in with a kind smile and posed a question that would resonate deeply within me: "Why did you decide to come to West Point?" His voice held a note of familiarity, and there was a glimmer of recognition in his eyes. It was none other than Sean Astin, the actor who had portrayed Rudy in the movie that had inspired me during my darkest days.

Time seemed to pause as our worlds intersected. I shared my story with him, recounting the trials I had faced and the unyielding determination that had carried me to West Point. Sean Astin listened with unwavering attention, his words echoing with genuine admiration. We conversed not only about my journey but also about the universal themes of courage and perseverance that had guided both of us.

Over the years, we stayed in touch. He became a mentor and a friend, providing support and encouragement as I continued to break barriers and inspire others. Our connection was a testament to the power of dreams, determination, and the remarkable bonds that can emerge from the most unexpected encounters. I realized no challenge is insurmountable with courage and perseverance.

Remember, in the most challenging moments of our lives, it is often the darkest hours that reveal our brightest strengths. May my story be a testament to the remarkable potential that exists within us all, waiting to be awakened by the trials and tribulations we face. Our courage knows no bounds, and our perseverance can move mountains.

As you navigate the winding paths of your own journey, always remember that within you, there is a light that can pierce even the darkest shadows.

CaS Facciponti is a West Point graduate and retired US Army officer. She is the founder of Alpaca Your Trauma, a nonprofit that uses ecotherapy to support the healing of Veterans and their families. CaS was named a Department of Veterans Affairs Women Trailblazer (2021). Currently, CaS is pursuing a PhD in Performance Psychology.

AlpacaYourTrauma.org

AWAKENING
TO PURPOSE:
A JOURNEY OF
SPIRITUAL DISCOVERY

Barry McFarlane

I'd just lost my job, the second in less than two years, and I was feeling down. I was definitely at a low point in my life.

The year was 2021. I'd been visiting my favorite sports bar three or four times a week. It's the kind of place where everyone knows your name, and since it's a sports bar, there's always a game on. So, I'd stop in for a couple of drinks and dinner. I was what you'd call a "regular."

The culmination of weekly drinking finally caught up with me, and I noticed I was feeling warm and lightheaded. As I got up from the bar stool to go to the restroom to splash water on my face, everything went dark.

Boom! I hit the floor; I passed out.

When I came to, all I could think about was my maternal grandfather, Jonas. Although I'd never met him, I knew he, too, was a "regular" and had met his end on the floor in a bar restroom in Jamaica.

Am I headed down that same path? I wondered.

My Guardian Angel

Amid the chaotic symphony of voices, one stood out like a beacon of solace. Soft and caring, it emanated from a woman kneeling by my side.

"You're going to be okay," she said. "The paramedics are on their way."

And with that, the paramedics arrived, strapped me to the gurney, and put me in the ambulance. As we raced toward the emergency room, the paramedic asked: "Barry, can you hear me?"

"Yes."

"You're severely dehydrated," he explained. "The alcohol you've consumed has caught up with you, destabilizing your electrolyte levels and causing you to pass out."

I nodded.

"We're administering an IV to replenish your fluids and restore your body's balance."

"Okay. Thanks for explaining what happened."

Barry, you need to change your ways, or you'll end up like your grandfather!

This was one heck of a wake-up call. Yet something about this experience seemed oddly familiar.

Catalyst for Transformation

Nearly twenty-seven years ago to the day, I'd been working in Sydney, Australia, diligently fulfilling my role as a financial consultant for a global shipping and mailing company that provided technology, logistics, and financial services to more than 90 percent of Fortune 500 companies.

At the time, I was thirty-nine years old, a single, corporate business grunt, well-accustomed to the relentless grind of my profession. I was known for working and playing hard.

I'd long known of the therapeutic benefits of massage and regularly used it to equalize stress and heal my body. So, at the end of my work week, I asked the hotel's concierge to arrange a massage for me.

That's when I met Anne—a remarkable woman who would redefine my life and serve as the catalyst for a profound personal and professional transformation.

Inner World Awareness

Our first session together was the usual one-hour, deep-tissue massage. However, it was unlike any massage experience I'd ever had.

Lying on her table, feeling her strong hands kneading the kinks in my muscles, I was transported to a place deep within. A place I'd not visited before— my inner world! And being there for the first time, I knew instantly that I wanted to experience more and learn more. A seed was planted for sure.

After I dressed, I couldn't wait to talk with Anne.

"Anne, that was incredible!"

"Thank you." She smiled.

"It was unlike anything I've ever experienced. What did you do?"

"I listened to your body, allowing it to guide me on where to focus and what techniques to use," Anne explained.

"You mean physically?"

"Yes, but mostly energetically."

Although I didn't understand what that meant, my perspective on massage had shifted.

Awakening to Purpose

In 1994, I spent most of my time in Sydney, a year marked by significant events that profoundly impacted my life, from the O.J. Simpson trial to the heart-wrenching loss of my beloved New York Knicks in the NBA championships. It was also the year my paternal grandfather passed away while I was on the other side of the planet.

Throughout it all, I continued my sessions with Anne. As we spent more time together, I discovered she was more than just a massage therapist—she was a Reiki master, spiritual empath, and psychic.

During one of our final sessions, Anne conducted a psychic reading and channeled her spiritual guides. Channeling was a wholly new and eye-opening experience for me. As we sat facing each other, she guided me into a meditative state and invited her guides in. The message they conveyed was powerful:

"Barry, you're not following your soul's purpose."

Not following my purpose? What the heck did that mean? I was a single, corporate climber busy chasing after more. Who has time to think about their soul's purpose?

The guides did not stop there but went on to reveal that my true purpose was that of a teacher or healer. They told me I would have children who would play a significant role later in my life. I was a bit mystified, especially with the prediction of children.

But the role of healer resonated with me given the profound impact of Anne's work on my body, mind, and spirit. I understood that I'd been navigating life without a clear direction—sleepwalking in an unfulfilled life. This powerful realization awakened within me a longing for a deeper, more purposefully lived life.

Words of Wisdom

By the time I left Sydney, I knew my purpose was to help others through massage and energy work. And with that, Anne imparted her final bits of wisdom: "Barry, always pay attention to your guides and your intuition. Listen more to your heart than your mind."

Upon returning to the United States, I enrolled in massage school and became a licensed massage therapist in 1997. I worked as a financial businessman by day and a massage therapist by night.

Thinking back on my time in Sydney, I'm amazed by how what a transformational year it was. Not only did it serve as my initial wake-up call, but it also propelled me on a path of spiritual discovery and purposeful living.

Life In-Between

A lot of life happened between 1998 and 2021 when I found myself lying passed out on the bar floor. I'd navigated two marriages and divorces, bought and sold four homes, and faced more job losses than I'd like to recount.

True to the psychic reading, my first daughter entered the world when I was forty-eight, followed by the arrival of my second daughter when I was fifty. They became integral parts of my life, shaping my experiences and perspectives.

Sadly, I stopped being a massage therapist when my oldest was born, and after that, my life became a roller coaster of joys and losses. Once again, I was far from my soul's purpose . . . until that day in November when I collapsed on the bar floor! That was my *second* wake-up call, urging me to realign with my soul's purpose.

Getting Back on Track

A few days after that experience, a friend introduced me to the teachings of energy intuitive and channeler Lee Harris.[2]

I began listening to Lee daily and registered for his annual Rebirth seminar in 2022.

I felt magic returning to my life as my heart and mind unified in spirit. I was reawakening to my purpose. And as a result, life got easier, I found meaningful work, and best of all—I called in my soulmate, Sarina.

Sarina

At the age of sixty-eight, I met Sarina.

I'd been divorced for a decade and had given up on finding true love. But the universe had other plans.

---

2 "Lee Harris," accessed November 13, 2023, https://www.leeharrisenergy.com.

In 2022, my inner world prompted me to imagine a new, different love story—one that I'd not experienced that would complement me in every way. So, I signed up for a subscription on a dating app and submitted my profile.

I was thoughtful and intentional about the information I included, knowing, with absolute certainty, that I wanted to call in my soulmate. And I did!

From the start, the attraction was immediate, and the connection intensely familiar.

We discovered that we'd lived close to each other as children, graduated from the same university, and shared a deep interest in metaphysical matters.

We both were followers of Lee Harris, had attended the same 2022 Rebirth seminar, and had already signed up for his next one.

In all ways that matter to us, Sarina and I are aligned. And when we're together, it feels like home.

Today, Sarina and I share a deep love and a commitment to a future fueled by our collective desire to join our soul's purpose to help and heal others.

As we embark on this journey, our enthusiasm for what lies ahead is palpable. Awakened to our soul's purpose, we embrace the transformative power of love.

 **Barry McFarlane** and his multi-lifetime partner, Sarina Arcari, are co-founders of The O+Positive Way. Together, they share lessons on walking the path toward elevating your personal vibration, calling in the love and life you desire, and co-creating conscious union with a divine counterpart. Visit The O+Positive Way website to join their heart-guided community.

OPositiveWay.com

OUR TIME:
A HIGHER-FREQUENCY
LOVE STORY

Sarina Arcari

How is this my life?

This is a question that echoes through my mind as I find myself in the most unexpected and enchanting chapter of my life's journey. It's a Sunday evening in early autumn 2023, and I am on the precipice of an experience that defies explanation.

The room dances in the soft glow of candles, and I'm about to receive a massage that will move me beyond the ordinary and into the realm of the extraordinary.

For over three decades, therapeutic massage has been a faithful companion in my quest for wellness. Skilled therapists have come and gone, each leaving their mark, but tonight is different.

Magical Experience

As I lie down on the massage table, Barry asks: "Any area that you'd like me to focus on?"

"I trust you to go wherever your intuition guides you," I reply.

He smiles.

As I settle onto the table, the energies in the room begin to shift, and the physical and metaphysical boundaries blur.

Barry begins. His touch is already resonating at a higher frequency of vibration. The synergy between us is electric.

When it ends, I'm nearly speechless.

"That was magical," I say.

"For me, too."

Who Is This Man?

Wrapped in the afterglow of one of the most magical massages I've ever had, I sit quietly, absorbing the atmosphere. Around me, I see candlelight reflecting off warm surfaces. I hear heart chakra music playing in the background. Looking outside, the moonlight is dancing on the Bay.

Inside, I feel a deep love and higher frequency connection with this extraordinary man I've known—maybe across many lifetimes—and I whisper "Thank you" to the universe for guiding us together again.

Barry, whom I've only known—this time around— for three months, is an Ivy League-educated accountant, trained massage therapist, and now my later-in-life soulmate.

I'm sixty.

Barry is sixty-eight.

How is it possible that we're experiencing this kind of love in our sixties?

We know it's our time.

Me? Use a Dating App?

It was the middle of May 2023. I was engrossed in finalizing a complex, multi-stop flight booking for an upcoming business trip to the Middle East. Frustration grew as an incessant pop-up advertisement kept interrupting my concentration. I clicked it off once, twice, and at least ten more times before I wondered if the universe was trying to get my attention.

The next time, it popped up. I paused.

A dating app for people over fifty!

"Good grief!" I exclaimed. *Enough of this!* Click.

And right back it came.

"Okay. Okay!"

Begrudgingly, I clicked on the advertisement and immediately felt the nudge from my inner knower to explore further—which was the last thing I wanted to do! I just wasn't feeling certain about getting into the dating game, especially online, at this point in life.

So much for that!

Before I knew it, I was signing up for their one-month membership.

"Fine. One month, that's it," I told the universe.

I started my profile, entered my credit card information, and uploaded a few carefully selected photos. Although I was reluctant, I did attempt to craft an intriguing but honest profile that highlighted some recent adventures I'd had and would hopefully magnetize the type of man I was seeking. I found out later that Barry also had been very intentional about writing his profile, also wanting to attract the right person.

After answering the suggested questions and setting the parameters for the men I wanted to meet, I pressed "submit" and went to sleep.

Que Será, Será

After that, I took a *que será, será* approach to the dating app, deciding what would be would be.

I'd pay attention to whomever "liked" me, but I wouldn't actively pursue men. A few "likes" trickled into my account over the next few days, but none piqued my interest.

I left for my business trip to the Middle East about ten days later. While there, I realized I couldn't access the dating app. No biggie. I was busy with board meetings and events anyway.

Famous Last Words

I returned to the United States in mid-June without giving that app another thought until, three days later, I received notification that I'd soon be billed for the second month's subscription.

Oh no, you don't.

Determined to cancel my membership, I logged into the app, and the app's "suggested match for today" caught my eye—a handsome man, casually dressed, with a beach in the background of his photo. There was something about him that intrigued me.

With three days to go, I thought, *There's no harm in scrolling through his profile, Sarina.*

Famous last words!

Every word he had written drew me in. Every picture he'd uploaded intrigued me further. Then came the clincher in the very last words of his profile— we'd attended the same university!

"Seriously, universe?"

I sent him a text.

He responded.

We quickly discovered that we'd shared professors and classes when we were each in our twenties. I knew where his dorm had been and he mine. And we're both still fans of the alma mater's teams more than forty years later!

No Holding Back

We met for lunch on June 24, five weeks after I finally clicked on that pesky pop-up. I felt his energy enter the restaurant before I saw him. And when he entered, it was as if no one else was in the room except him.

Our conversation flowed effortlessly; we discovered many more things in common, and we were both heady with excitement. Three hours later—we hardly noticed the time—I invited Barry to my place to watch the Fourth of July fireworks.

Over the summer, our connection deepened; we spent nearly every weekend together and talked every day. Our compatibility was magical, and our trust was complete. "No holding back" became our mantra. We knew we'd known each other in other lifetimes—how else could this magnetically familiar force be explained?

For both of us, it felt like home when we were in each other's arms.

From Dark Night to Candlelight

Here's the interesting thing: I had known Barry was coming to me. No, not Barry, the person—Barry, the soul.

114

It was September 2022. Eight months before the advertisements started popping up on my computer screen. I was living alone in Hawaii, single-handedly finishing up the renovations of my parents' home there, experiencing a "dark night of the soul" as the end of my sixtieth year approached.

I'd recently left a thirty-year corporate career, suddenly landed halfway across the planet when my parents were both hospitalized, and subsequently ended a long-distance personal relationship.

This can't be my life!

I recognized my need for comprehensive transformation in every facet of my life. Living alone in my childhood home, with all its memories, only intensified the urgency for healing. I was doing everything I knew to elevate my mind, body, and spirit, adding energy work, light wave therapy, herbal remedies, and sound wave healing. I vacillated regularly between hope and despair, five thousand miles away from my own home.

During this time, I journaled daily about what I was experiencing while, at the same time, writing about the life I desired to manifest. Always, I felt the presence of Barry.

On three separate nights, just before falling asleep, I was visited by a man calling for me—an enigmatic man of color, his features veiled, beckoning me with an outstretched hand saying, "Come on, baby."

I felt as though I already knew him. He was familiar, and I felt comfortable and at ease in his presence. Although I couldn't see his face, intuitively, I knew— he was my soulmate.

One day, as I was journaling about the man I wanted in my life, emphatically, I added to my journal: "I want a man who can give an expert massage!"

And so it is…

That September 25, 2022, journal entry became my reality nine months later when I met Barry.

Higher-Frequency Love Story

Reflecting on my life now, I'm moved by the transformative journey that has led me to this moment. What began with a "dark night of the soul" in Hawaii unfolded into a beautiful manifestation nine months later with Barry giving me an expert massage by candlelight.

And while our love story came into being with a simple click on a dating app, we know it began much earlier as a higher-frequency love story we both had been summoning long before our paths officially crossed.

With Barry, I've come to realize that time is an illusion, and therefore, it simply is not possible to run out of something that does not exist. Love adheres to no restrictions, it unfolds in its own time, and soulmates materialize when *we* are truly ready. We are never "too old," and it is never "too late" to call in the love and life of our dreams.

 **Sarina Arcari** and her multi-lifetime partner, Barry McFarlane, are co-founders of The O+Positive Way. Together, they share lessons on walking the path toward elevating your personal vibration, calling in the love and life you desire, and co-creating conscious union with a divine counterpart. Visit The O+Positive Way website to join their heart-guided community.

OPositiveWay.com

STOP, DROP, AND ROLL
IN THE
NAME OF LOVE!
Veronica L. Nabizadeh, Esq.

There I was, on my knees, clutching my daughter to my chest.

Weeping.

I had failed to do what every mother swears to do—protect my daughter. My world lay shattered in pieces around me.

In two words, the great job I'd prided myself in doing ceased to exist. I'd been a fool. Children always know. The secret I thought I'd protected Kara from had been exposed.

There was no pretending it hadn't happened and no replay button to press.

Kara's two words laid me bare. And while I was mortified to my core, shamed by my behavior, and embarrassed that it had come to this, I vowed I'd make things right.

What you're about to read isn't pretty. But it's truth—in the name of love.

Our First Date

It all began twenty-three years ago when I was working at a dating service, and my boss, Marianne, came into my office and asked, "Are you willing to go on a date with a new client?"

"A date? I thought dating clients was against corporate policy," I said.

"It is," she answered. "However, we have such a shortage of women in our dating pool that we're unable to provide a large enough selection for our VIP clients."

"So, you're asking your staff to fill in?"

"No. Just you."

"Me? Why me?" I asked.

"He bought a Gold VIP package and hasn't approved of *any* of the women candidates we selected for him," Marianne replied.

"And you think I'd be a good fit?"

"Yes. He's a physician."

A physician? I'd always wanted to marry a doctor. My breath caught.

"Let me see his file."

Later that afternoon, I opened the file of Shahriar A. Nabizadeh. And even before I got to the end, I was smitten!

Tall: check.

Dark: check (Persian).

Green eyes: check!

Educated: check.

Potential for financial stability: check.

Likes the Dallas Cowboys: yes, check!

Looking for a tall, brunette professional or career-minded woman with a degree: yep, that's me!

We talked on the phone for weeks about everything and agreed to meet at a bougie restaurant in the historic district of San Marcos for our first date.

Inside, well-dressed couples were sipping wine, and jazz played in the background—Café on the Square was chic!

With only twenty dollars to my name and not knowing if Shahriar would pick up the tab, I gulped when the waiter handed me the menu—every entrée was more than twenty dollars! Oh-oh. So, I ordered a bowl of soup and a glass of water.

Inexplicably, Shahriar ordered the same.

Crickets

The waiter brought the soup, and we both tucked in. Conversation flowed all around us, yet we ate in silence. The voice inside my head piped up:

- Is this a cultural thing?
- Do Persians eat their meals in silence?
- Did he only order soup because he wanted to get our date over with?

Marianne had said he hadn't found any woman he liked at the dating service, I reminded myself. *Let's wrap this date up and get out of here!*

"Dinner" was finished.

The server cleared the table, then asked if we wanted dessert.

"No."

"No."

That was it. Our first date was over in twenty minutes.

Nine months later, we were married!

February 19, 2000

The ceremony took place in my husband's brother's formal living room, and I walked down the hallway on my dad's arm to Pachelbel's *Canon in D.*

Shahriar sat waiting by the traditional *Sofreh Aghd* my mother had beautifully arranged on a gorgeous Persian rug.

I felt beautiful, alive, and happy as I approached him.

"You look breathtaking."

"And so do you," I replied.

The Mullah performed the ceremony in Farsi, and since I didn't understand a word, I had to ask *three* times if we were, for real, married.

(Okay, dear reader, I know. Three times is excessive. But the budding lawyer in me had to make sure!)

Our immediate family and two of Shahriar's college buddies were in attendance; there were thirty people in all.

It was romantic and intimate.

I was married to the man of my dreams.

From the moment Marianne asked me to go out on a date with Shahriar, it felt as though we were destined to be, as if fate or a higher power had brought us together. And tonight would consecrate that promise.

I couldn't wait to be alone with Shahriar!

And then I wasn't.

(Insert record scratch.)

Shahriar had just announced his plans to return to his brother's house to take care of his two college buddies.

"Shahriar, it's our wedding night. Don't you want to be with me?"

"Of course I do, but my brothers need me to make sure my friends get home safely," he replied.

Really? No one else could help them home?

"But what about me? What about us?"

Shahriar hesitated before responding. "I'm sorry."

And just like that, as I lay there clutching his pillow, the seed of codependency, which had lay dormant for years, sprouted.

The Beginning of the End

Shahriar and I started fighting soon after our wedding—no surprise.

Things had changed between us. The kind, attentive, caring man I'd fallen in love with was still there, but it was now entangled with the complex dance of codependency we'd orchestrated. The needier I became, the more distant he was.

Our fighting escalated.

Shahriar and I were locked in a power struggle, one-upping each other daily. I ended up depressed and anxious. I rarely left the house. I was a shell of my robust, energetic, pre-marriage happy self.

And Shahriar?

He was sullen and even more withdrawn.

Slayed by Truth

My down-on-my-knees-weeping moment came when Kara was four years old.

Shahriar and I had been fighting, and I was busy pretending it hadn't happened when she came into the kitchen with crocodile tears in her eyes, pleading: "Mommy, please stop. You and Daddy fight all the time!"

Oh no!

Despite our best efforts to fight in private, Kara knew what was happening and needed me to make it stop.

Please stop! Instantly, those two words slayed me and turned me into a failure as a mother.

Mothers are supposed to protect their children. They're supposed to provide a safe place to thrive, a nurturing environment to feel loved, and a harmonious home in which to live.

I hadn't.

Worse still, my self-absorbed, needy self hadn't provided the one thing Kara needed most— peace.

Please stop!

(Those two words still haunt me.)

Yet, as I bear-hugged Kara to me, I vowed to stop fighting and start figuring things out.

Stop, Drop, and Roll

Do you recall the simple fire safety technique children are taught to minimize damage if their clothing catches on fire: Stop, Drop, and Roll?

They're told to stop, ceasing any movement that fans the flames. Then they should drop to the ground and cover their faces with their hands to avoid injury. Finally, they're to roll on the ground or wrap themselves up with a rug to deprive the fire of oxygen, thus extinguishing the flames.

Well, that technique works when couples are on fire, too.

From the moment I heard Kara's plea, I decided to:

1. Stop contributing to the fighting. Stop one-upping my husband. And stop escalating the arguments.
2. Drop my neediness to avoid further injury when Shahriar distanced himself.
3. Roll myself in inner wholeness to deprive our arguments of oxygen.

Easy-peasy, right?

(I know you're chuckling with me.)

Fortified with the image of Kara's tear-streaked face and the echo of her plea, I did it.

Much to Shahriar's surprise—and mine, too—I fought with him less. I reduced my salvo of needy behaviors while learning techniques to strengthen my inner wholeness.

Dear reader, I'd love to tell you this was an easy thing to do. But it wasn't.

There were many, *many* times that I didn't stop. Didn't drop. Didn't roll. But I didn't give up. After a good cry, and with Kara's voice ringing in my ears, I'd pick myself up and stop, drop, and roll again.

Whenever I felt like giving up and throwing in the towel, I reminded myself why I was doing this— for Kara. I wanted Kara to grow up to be a strong, confident woman. Secure in herself, bold in her decisions, and at peace within her environment.

I wanted to model for her the courageous woman I would become.

Courageous Act of Marriage

Kara is now thirteen, and Shahriar and I have been married for twenty-three years.

Stop, drop, and roll in the name of love saved our marriage, and it's why our family thrives and flourishes.

It also launched me as a courageous woman on fire for truth in the name of love, helping other battle-weary wives boldly and confidently make their decisions.

Getting married is the easy part. Working through the challenging aspects and thriving beyond them to the sweet love of companionship awaiting is what takes courage.

Be courageous. Much is awaiting you in the name of love.

Veronica L. Nabizadeh, Esq. owner of Relationship Restart, helps battle-weary wives with children who face marital challenges when their husbands resist going to therapy. Her experience navigating marital challenges fuels her passion and gives courage to others. Veronica shares her life with her husband, Shahriar, and Kara, their wise, old-soul daughter.

RelationshipRestart.net

COURAGE
TO
INSPIRE

Shahriar A. Nabizadeh, MD

My dad had a green thumb.

Growing up in Tehran, we had a large garden behind our house where Dad grew herbs and vegetables and experimented with grafting roses. One of his most impressive results was a rose bush with four different colors of roses!

Dad was an agricultural engineer, and he was one of the lucky ones of his generation who got to do for work what he was passionate about doing in life—caring for plants.

Grafting roses is part precision and part hoping for the best. Mid-summer, as soon as the bloom had begun to fade, Dad carefully selected the bud he would graft onto the rootstock plant (another rose bush). Taking his knife, he'd cut an inch-long "T" into the rootstock, peel open the flaps, and insert the base of the bud between the flaps. He'd close the flaps around the bud, wrap it in grafting tape, water it, and hope for the best.

Dad's creativity and endless curiosity was passed down to all us kids. And he never stopped caring for his plants.

My two brothers, sister, and I inherited Dad's passion for caring. No wonder we chose the professions we did.

Cultural Values

Being a physician is highly valued in Iran, as is being an educator.

So, when my eldest brother was born, my parents were on a mission to ensure he got a good education and became a physician.

He scored the highest grade on the national rigorous Konkur examination after high school and entered Tehran University Medical School. He followed that by being at the top of the national medical school graduate class. He received a medal from the Shah of Iran and was awarded a full scholarship to continue his path in medicine in the United States.

It was quite an honor for him and a proud moment for our family.

So, off my brother went to make his mark as a neurologist.

And right behind him was my second-eldest brother, who came to America to become a pulmonary critical care physician.

In between my two brothers was my sister, who came to America and became a Montessori teacher.

Groomed from Birth

As a child, I knew I was being groomed to follow in my brothers' footsteps.

But I had other interests, too, such as philosophy and physics. Everything about the cosmos fascinated me. If left to my own devices, I might have become an astrophysicist, looking into space through telescopes and collecting data from space probes to discover how the universe works.

Or I could have been a drummer.

But that's another story.

I came to America and enrolled in the College of William and Mary as a pre-med student with a double major in biology and physics and a minor in philosophy.

I couldn't help myself—I was interested in so many things!

Sadly, no music minor.

I ultimately, specialized in physical medicine and rehabilitation and currently am the medical director of an inpatient rehabilitation system in Florida.

And now, thirty years later, I know why—so I could collaborate with patients.

Looking back, I see that I inherited my dad's passion for creativity in addition to his caring.

Treating the Other 90 Percent

In my field of medicine, creativity is essential. I often become a place of hope for patients seeking radical transformation. They come to me with the desire to feel better and improve their functionality, despite the limitations of their illness.

When they get to my inpatient rehabilitation unit, these patients' bodies and minds are completely beaten, tapped out, and drained by the disease process and treatments. The trauma of the drastic loss and change in their lives has left them with little hope of regaining their health and joy of living.

After other specialists have done their best by focusing on the visible 10 percent of the "health iceberg" above, my approach must address the crucial 90 percent below. I see my patients as more than their illnesses; I consider their whole person.

Whenever I meet a new patient, I ask myself, "Can I inspire them to take greater responsibility for their health?"

During our interactions, I explore their past traumas, current living environment, family dynamics, and support system. We engage in meaningful dialogue about their commitment to healing, seeking to understand their level of buy-in to recovery and wellness.

"Will you take ownership of your part in both the disease and its solution?" is the question I ask my patients. Their response provides invaluable insight into their readiness to participate in the treatment plan.

At this point, courage becomes paramount for the patients.

This is because under my care, they are not mere observers; they become actively involved in their healing journey. After all, it is their health we are working to restore, and their commitment plays a significant role in achieving the best possible outcome.

Awakening the Passive Patient

As you might expect, patients are a bit taken aback by my approach.

Because no one has asked them to tap into the reality of what makes them succeed in healing, they look like deer in headlights for the first two sessions. And since no one has held them responsible for their success, they don't know how to respond to a physician who does.

Who could blame them?

Every patient has been through the wringer by the time their path crosses mine. Every specialist has done their best to correct the patient's illness. But no one has asked anything of them.

I ask.

As a result, patients have become passive travelers within a healthcare system that treats their symptoms without looking at them as a whole person.

I do.

You may have heard of the Mayo Clinic. They're the worldwide leader in providing expert, whole-person care to everyone who needs treatment. Their team of doctors evaluate and develop care plans tailored to each patient.

Well, I see the body as the ultimate healthcare plan.

Most patients are shocked by and in awe of their body's true capacity. They appreciate having a physician who helps them understand what's happening, love the connection they have with me, and value the genuine rapport we build.

Crazy to Care

Some might consider me crazy for caring so deeply, and maybe I am, but it nourishes my heart.

Just like in college, where my curiosity led me to explore various interests, the same applies to healthcare—wholeheartedly caring is natural to me; resisting it is out of the question.

Caring for the whole person is not just a job; it's my passion. And when patients get that, it awakens a shared sense of purpose, propelling me to care even more.

Call me crazy, but nothing compares to the overwhelming joy I feel when I know I've done everything I can to meet my patients' needs, whether they fully embrace it or not.

Radical Care

To each of you reading this chapter, I want you to know that when you become a patient, you deserve the comprehensive and compassionate care I'm talking about.

- You *should* expect and demand more from your doctor; in turn, they should expect more from you. Healthcare between physician and patient is an amazing collaborative experience. And if it isn't, it needs to be.
- When you enter into a relationship with a physician, there must be genuine care from both sides—they for you and, just as importantly, you for them!
- Trust is paramount in this relationship, and even if you don't fully trust your doctor yet, be open to developing that trust over time.

- Honest communication is essential, with both parties actively listening, asking questions, and speaking truth to each other. Your quality of life should be at the heart of all treatment plans, and your active involvement is crucial for success.

I'm describing radical, whole-person care—a return to the kind of attention that used to be the mainstay of the medical profession. And that is still here in physicians like me who care not just for the one rose, but like my father before me, for the whole garden.

Courage to Inspire

In my role as a physician, I'm steadfast in my belief that patients possess an innate power to heal. While the healthcare system can offer invaluable support, it should not be the sole pillar upon which patients lean. Instead, I champion patients to actively foster a deep and meaningful bond with their physicians, a relationship that extends beyond mere prescriptions, diagnostic tests, and infrequent six-month checkups.

As physicians, we need to go beyond the textbook knowledge acquired in medical school and harness our empathetic and empathic nature. As mentors and guides on our patients' healing journey, we need to illuminate their path with education and tailored treatments. Together, we can champion their comprehensive well-being, transforming their recovery into a shared, passionate endeavor.

Patients, I implore you to look for a physician who inspires you to be courageous. To view your body as an incredible healing machine, your heart as its compass, and your mind as fertile ground for positivity, clarity, and mindfulness. Realize and harness your inherent capacity for healing—together, you and your physician can achieve remarkable outcomes!

Shahriar A. Nabizadeh, MD, is a healer, mentor, visionary, and health strategist for patients seeking radical, whole-person transformation. He encourages patients to take responsibility for their health and inspires them to be courageous. Shahriar shares his life with his wife, Veronica, daughter Kara, and their two dogs, William and Mary.

PersonalRestart.com

THEY HAPPEN
TO
CALL ME MOM

Debra Poneman

The year was 1988, and I was at the top of my game. I was traveling the United States, giving my Yes to Success seminars in cities from coast-to-coast, and I had reps teaching in nine countries on four continents. The first infomercial in the history of infomercials to offer a self-improvement product was my twelve-cassette *Yes to Success* program. My book manuscript was in the hands of one of the biggest agents in the country who already had interest from coveted New York publishers—and I was in negotiations for my own TV talk show.

Then, on the evening of July 5, after the fireworks had been put away and "Stars and Stripes Forever" was no longer ringing in our ears, I made the decision to give it all up—the book, the show, the seminars, the infomercial—because, that night, I met a teacher who showed me what success was really all about.

I had spent years studying with some of the greatest gurus, spiritual masters, and transformational leaders of our time. But this teacher was different. Her name was Deanna, although we didn't know that yet, and she came into the world at 7:42 p.m. From the moment the midwife placed her on my chest, and I saw that little scrunched-up face, I was swept away—not only because she was my baby, but because I was now holding my very own eight-pound truth barometer.

When she looked up at me, those eyes saw right into my soul. I knew at that moment that the jig was up, that I could no longer be the *personality* Debra—I now had to be the *person* Debra. I could no longer get away with doing things like telling little expedient lies or not being my word or walking my talk. Those eyes saw me—the good, the bad, and the ugly—and through them, I saw myself.

Although my plan was to give birth and get back to spreading the message of success throughout the world, the core of my teaching was to follow the impulses of your heart. Yep, with all the assuredness of an evangelical preacher, I had told the world that even if your heart appears to be leading you in the opposite direction of your goals, if you want true success, you have to trust those impulses. On that fateful day, the impulses of my heart were saying it was time for my career to come to a screeching halt—and I made the decision to become a full-time stay-at-home mom.

I exchanged my seats in the business-class cabin for a seat on the floor in the kinder-gym, my chic business attire for overalls that could be thrown up on, and my brilliant speeches on how to create a life of success for brilliant speeches on why you should share your toys and eat your broccoli. The most astounding part was that I never got even one round of applause, and I thought my speeches were really very compelling.

But the reality was that I was no longer the sole authority on all things success. There was a new success expert in town, and the lessons were coming fast and furiously.

One of my very first memorable lessons was imparted when Deanna was around four. I was pushing her in a stroller when we passed a beautiful rose garden and I exclaimed, "Can you believe God created something as beautiful as a rose? He is the most amazing artist." To which she replied without skipping a beat, "How do you know God is a he?" Needless to say, being the consummate feminist I purported to be, I immediately backpedaled and explained that God has no gender, and what I meant to say was "He or she." But Deanna would have none of my explanation and instead admonished me by saying, "Well, Mommy, if you meant 'he or she,' next time you shouldn't just say 'he.'" Lesson #1: Say what you mean, and if you screw up, admit it.

As she got older, it only got worse—or I guess you could say better. When Deanna was in her early twenties, she became a personal stylist at Nordstrom, and she was fantastic at it. I remember the day when she said to me out of the blue, "By the way, Mom, I know you're disappointed in me that I'm not saving starving children or teaching meditation and that I'm just a stylist." To which I replied, "Deanna, you are soooo wrong. I'm totally proud of you."

But, as usual, Deanna would have none of it, and in her no-BS-allowed manner said, "I'll let you live your delusion, but I hear how you apologize to your friends when you tell them I'm a stylist. But I want you to know, Mom, that when I bring someone into my styling room who has thought for her entire life that she was unattractive or even ugly, and I pick out the right clothes and right jewelry, and I hold up her hair, and she turns around and looks in the mirror and sees herself as beautiful for the first time, I change just as many lives as you do." Lesson #2: Everyone's work is important. We all change lives in our own way. Everyone deserves our respect.

And then there is Deanna's little brother, born three years later, who also came out of the womb with an innate sense of integrity. When Daniel was around three or four, he turned to me one day and innocently asked, "Why do your friends say, 'Love you!' to someone and then say bad things about them after they leave?" Good one, Daniel! Even as a child, he noticed hypocrisy and couldn't understand it—and more often than I care to admit, he sniffed it out in me.

When Daniel was in eighth grade, his entire class went on a trip to Washington, DC. For weeks before the trip, the boys were busy planning their antics, including how they were going to sneak into the girls' rooms in the hotel and pick up chicks on the National Mall. I never heard much talk about the Lincoln Memorial or Washington Monument.

Two nights before the departure, all the parents attended the obligatory meeting where we were to receive the essential trip details. The last item of business was the room assignments. First, all the girls' rooms were read out and then the boys' rooms. The teacher announced, "And in room number one, we have Asher, Max, Ke'juan, and Terrance."

That's interesting, I thought, *those are Daniel's four closest friends.*

The teacher continued, "And in room number two will be Stefano, Jacob, Teddy, and Donte."

Wait, I thought, *those are Daniel's other closest friends.*

The teacher got to the end of the list—and no Daniel. Just as I was about to get up and ask why he'd been left off the list, or more accurately, what he'd done now, the teacher added, "Oh, and

Daniel Poneman will be in a room with Eric and Eric's personal aide."

Now, to be honest, my heart sank. Daniel's assigned roommates were an autistic boy and a not-too-hip man in his thirties. Although I loved Eric with all my heart, and Daniel did too—he'd been over to the house many times—my first thought was that Daniel was going to be disappointed. How was I going to break this news to him?

As I was driving home, I struggled with my dilemma. If he were really upset, what would I do?

So, I got home and walked into the den. I started out by telling Daniel about the swimming pool at the hotel, and then I mustered the courage to share the roommate news. "Honey," I said, "the roommates were assigned, and I want you to know that if you're really upset, maybe I can call Ms. Culver and see what we can arrange, but they put you in a room with Eric and his personal aide."

At that point, Daniel looked at me with a quizzical look on his face and said, "Mom, they didn't put me in a room with Eric—I asked to be with Eric. I realized if he wasn't with me, he'd get left out, and you know, Mom, it's his eighth grade class trip too."

So, yes, I've been blessed to sit at the feet of some of the greatest teachers and most enlightened gurus of our time, and I myself have been regarded as a changemaker by many, but if I had to say whose teachings have had the most profound and lasting impact on my life, I would have to say that without a doubt, it's been the teachings and the examples of those two changemaker gurus who happen to call me Mom.

The founder of Yes to Success, Inc., **Debra Poneman** is a bestselling author and internationally renowned success and anti-aging expert. Since 1981, she's empowered hundreds of thousands to live their dreams by providing a system for creating financial abundance, true inner and outer success, and the radiant health to support it.

YesToSuccess.com

FROM BETRAYAL
TO
BLESSINGS

Jaelee Richardson

We're all broken; that's how the light gets in.
—Ernest Hemmingway

Whenever I tell anyone the story I'm about to share with you, it feels as though I am dropping a bomb on them. I myself have had a hard time wrapping my head around the series of events that have led me here, about to take a leap of faith and pour out my heart to you. But through my journey to heal my broken heart, I've received so many blessings along the way that I wouldn't have had otherwise. I am a better person for having the courage to find healing and forgiveness.

The first time I had an inclination that something might be going on between Mr. Wrong and my older sister was the summer of 2014. To set the stage: I was gloriously pregnant in my last trimester, and we were at a family barbeque. I was sitting at a table in the shade with a full view of them playing horseshoes. My sister was overtly flirty, and I waited (prayed) for him to brush her off. Instead, I could see how much he was enjoying her attention. That was the first of many gut feelings. My sister's flirting with my man wasn't a shocker to me, but his reaction most certainly was.

My older sister and I are just two-and-a-half years apart, and she was truly my first friend in life. Even though Mr. Wrong and I never married, we had been together for several years, and when I got pregnant, we moved in together. Most people in my life at the time didn't understand our relationship or my attraction to him. At the time, he felt more like my Mr. Big than a Mr. Run as Fast as You Can. He was an older executive, and I was utterly charmed and ruthlessly love-bombed. I truly believed in my heart that he was the love of my life and we were meant to be together. I was a divorced single mom looking for my second chance at a happily ever after, and he painted an irresistible picture. Sometimes the hardest things to let go of aren't the physical things but the story we paint in our minds.

After I had my daughter, he really changed from Jekyll to Hyde, and our life together was on a downward spiral. I was no longer the center of his universe, and although he has always been a kind, doting father to our girl, he turned on me, and I wasn't emotionally prepared. Perhaps because my emotions were all over the place after having our daughter, I really bought into his gaslighting. Any concern or suspicion I had was dismissed, and I was made out to be delusional; the sad part was that I turned on myself and second-guessed my own sanity during that time.

When my daughter was just seven months old, I developed a large kidney stone that subsequently became infected. I was admitted to the hospital, where I got a good dose of Cipro, an antibiotic, to clear the infection. Unbeknownst to everyone, I had a severe allergy to that medication, and my organs began shutting down. Long story short, an angel of an ICU nurse figured it out, and after three weeks in the hospital, I was able to go home.

I remember checking in with Mr. Wrong and our daughter while I was hospitalized, and I heard my sister in the background! I questioned this, and I was made to feel crazy for even having such gross suspicions, but not long after that ordeal, he left me for good.

I felt sorry for myself, but I had to put on my big girl panties and figure out how to be the best mom I could to my two precious little girls. The first order of business was making sure I got custody of both girls so I could raise them together. Even though custody was shared, keeping them together was all I cared about.

Even though I believed no one would ever love me again and my life as I knew it was ruined, I pressed on. I had to pick up the pieces and just put one foot in front of the other.

Months later, I was scheduled to go to Florida for a work conference. I wanted to get my hair done beforehand, but my regular girl was unavailable. I reached out at the last minute to a stylist who happened to work at the same salon as my sister. As luck would have it, she had an opening for me. The moment I sat in her chair, the stylist looked me straight in my eyes with the oddest expression and said, "You know, it's so weird that you're here because I've been debating about whether or not to reach out to you."

The stylist knew my story; we're Facebook friends and she had seen my ex and knew what he looked like, so it was a surprise to her that he had been coming into the salon and getting close with my sister. She walked to my sister's drawer and pulled out a cell phone and told me it was my sister's "bat phone." My sister was still married to her second husband and didn't want him to see what she was up to.

When the stylist pulled out the phone, she showed me a text exchange between my sister and my ex, and my world as I knew it changed forever. The veil was lifted, and a line was drawn in the sand that there would never be any coming back from. I sobbed while I struggled to process the information. Within a few hours, I'd be on a plane one thousand miles away from everyone—with my first blessing ready and waiting for me.

Being in real estate for nearly two decades, I had been to many conferences; however, this was the first and only time they had hired a professional comedian to talk to us.[3] He had this bit about how you can make anything in your life funny if you just add a HAHAHA to the end of it. He had a few folks get up and talk about a seller who fired them or a time when another agent beat them on a listing and then add a big HAHAHA, and he had them all genuinely laughing. In my head, I said, "My ex and my sister are having an affair, HAHAHA," and it actually worked. I was cracking up. The comedian even said something like "the worse it is, the funnier." Surely there are certain things that will never be funny, but in my case, the first step in healing was having the ability to laugh about my situation. Laughter really is medicine!

When I shared my story early on with a coworker, she had quite an emotional reaction. She looked me in the eyes and said, "I would never forgive your sister," and I remember shaking my head in agreement at the time. But unless you've had the opportunity to live with betrayal and trauma and the heaviness of it, you may never understand that logically you have to

---

3 Craig Shuemaker, two-time Emmy Award-winning comedian and actor.

forgive if you are ever going to get rid of this weighted blanket of emotions. But how do you forgive?

It wasn't an easy process, and it didn't just come to me. I went to a Tony Robbins UPW and did the fire walk twice. I thought, *Hey, if I can unleash the power of mind over matter and walk across these coals without burning my feet, surely I can forgive these two.* While it was a fascinating and fun experience, my feelings were the same (and luckily so were my feet). I wasn't a stranger to therapy, and during that time I used all the resources available to me.

In my search for forgiveness, I came across something transformative in the Hawaiian practice of ho'oponopono. I allowed the simplicity of those four sentences to roll around over and over in my brain like a mantra: *I'm sorry, please forgive me, thank you, I love you.* I finally found the forgiveness I so desperately searched for when I realized I first had to forgive myself for going through the experience in the first place, something I'd never considered.

Once I was able to forgive myself, forgiving everyone else came naturally. I released the perfect picture I painstakingly painted in my brain and embraced the magic of what my life was turning into right in front of me: a thriving mom raising strong young women, my greatest blessings of all. In my search for forgiveness and healing, I had become someone new, a stronger yet more compassionate version that I wouldn't be had I not gone through this experience.

> *You either get bitter or you get better. It's that simple. You either take what has been dealt to you and allow it to make you a better person, or you allow it to tear you down. The choice does not belong to fate, it belongs to you.*
>
> —Josh Shipp

 **Jaelee Richardson** is an investor and entrepreneur who got her start in sales and transitioned into residential real estate, where she's been proudly serving clients for the last twenty years. Jaelee is a lifelong student of personal development and finds great purpose in making a difference in the lives of others as a mother, a realtor, and through her writing.

JaeleeRichardson.com

AWAKENING
TO
JOY

Safire Rose

Back in 1984, when I was twenty-seven, I underwent a profound shift in consciousness when I experienced, over the course of ten days, an inexplicable presence of joy that lifted me out of a life-threatening depression. That presence abides in me to this day. It forms the basis of my spiritual orientation to life and my approach to writing. Some might call my healing journey a breakdown; I call it a breakthrough. Some might call it a *spiritual emergency*, a term to describe a crisis of awakening and rebirth. For me, it was nothing short of a miracle.

Three years earlier, I'd broken up with my partner, Lindsey. That breakup brought up an uncontrollable anger. I didn't know how to process the anger, so I turned it inward and slipped into a deep depression. A friend recommended a therapist, Jessie, and for several months I went to therapy twice a week.

In therapy, I explored family patterns and identified the specifics of the grief behind my rage, including my father's desertion from the family when I was six. Still, I was overwhelmed by my pain, and that summer I tried to take my own life. My therapist suggested I enter a private psychiatric ward to keep myself safe, and I agreed.

For the first twenty-four hours, I was terrified. I was in a locked ward with others. I had no way to open the doors from the inside. Everything sharp was taken away from me. I felt alone and angry. Most of the social workers were frightened by my anger. Only one saw through it. His compassion quieted me.

After the twenty-four-hour hold, my month-long experience in the psych ward was healing. I learned how to set boundaries with others, and I talked to my family about my feelings in group therapy. I began to take care of myself. After I was released, I lived with my mother, stepfather, and brother. During that time, I had the sense that I would soon be in a relationship, and I was happy about the prospect.

A month later I met Christy. We started by going out dancing with friends, and later we fell in love. That love continues to this day. Although I was strong enough to begin a new relationship, I was in therapy three times a week to explore the roots of my anger and self-destructive thoughts. Two years later, Christy and I moved in together. Shortly after that, Christy received news that her father had a heart attack and was hospitalized. This turn of events catalyzed feelings of grief, abandonment, and rage within me.

I didn't know what to do. I felt desperate and alone, and I wondered if my sadness would ever go away. Although I wasn't consciously spiritual at the time, some seed of hope had been germinating inside me, and I remember saying out loud, "I just want to feel joy again." I wasn't sure to whom I was speaking, but I knew the words came from deep inside. It was as if I intuited another possibility but didn't know how to access it. Within the arc of those words, my whole life began to change, but I could not imagine what would happen next.

The next day I felt odd, but I went to work anyway. Christy was concerned and asked our neighbor Lynn to look in on me. When I got home, Lynn saw me walking down the driveway and went to meet me, but it was too late. Something had snapped, and my hold on what we understand as reality was slipping. My thinking was irrational, and although I knew I was still in the world, I had withdrawn into my own. I knew I needed help, so I contacted my therapist, and she urged me to come to her office immediately.

My therapist tried to snap me out of it, but I'd withdrawn too far. I'd regressed to the age of a four-year-old, and I had difficulties discerning what was real and what was not. I didn't have health insurance at the time, and I was terrified of going to the County

General hospital. My therapist had studied other models of healing, including network therapy, where the individual's community is involved in the process of therapy and healing. She also had a mentor diagnosed as schizophrenic who had returned to consensus reality.

My therapist knew I was part of a women's community, and she suggested that we try network therapy for one week. If I had been hospitalized, I would have been drugged and my experience labeled as pathological. Here was an opportunity for deeper healing. She told me that in order to implement the plan, I had to meet three conditions. First, I could not be a danger to myself or others. Second, I had to agree to come back to consensus reality a little each day. Third, I could not be alone. I also would continue therapy three times a week.

Even in my altered state, I knew Christy couldn't do everything. Her father was dying. Though I had regressed in age, I contacted others for help. My voice was like a small child's; inwardly I called myself "Little Me." I told people I was not well, that I had regressed in age, and I asked if they could help. Some of them thought I should be hospitalized, and some were afraid to see me. But many of those I asked had experienced alternative healing modalities themselves and agreed to help.

During that ten-day journey, thirty-five women sat with me in rotating shifts, 24/7. When I withdrew into myself, they brought me back by calling my name and grounding me. During each shift, I would ask my friend if they liked colors, numbers, or words. If a friend chose colors, we would finger-paint or color. If they chose numbers, we would play a game. If they chose words, we would read stories. One friend chose music, which delighted me, and we listened to music. I was highly intuitive at this time, and I told my friends about their lives. Many women told me later that it felt as though we were healing one another. This experience introduced me to the presence of joy. I felt whole, alive, and connected to life.

A few months later, I experienced memories of being molested by my father at an early age. I finally understood my chronic rage, and the puzzle pieces of my life began to fall together. Even today, as I traverse the ups and downs of daily living, I have access to the presence of joy that came into my awareness and into my life during that ten-day breakthrough. I learned that if I suppress an emotion, I suppress my joy. I now navigate life by allowing and experiencing all my emotions and discerning when (and when not) to act on them.

In 2002, I wrote the poem "She Let Go." I believe it contains the same energetic presence of joy and healing that lifted me out of my depression. The poem went viral, and every week I receive emails from around the world from individuals who have been touched by it in some way. The poem itself came quickly, but the person I had to become in order to write the poem took time.

I am now in my sixties. Since my breakthrough, I have not suffered suicidal thoughts or chronic depression. When challenges occur in my life, I access the presence of joy that resides inside me; I do the inner work necessary to change my attitude, and I move forward in my life.

The following keys keep me on track as a poet, author, and teacher. I hope they inspire you to grow spiritually and creatively.

1. *The power to change is within you.* Our inner attitude affects our outer experience. Declare your true desire, listen for guidance, and take inspired action toward your goals. Don't give up. Remember, who you are is more important than where you have been. If your personal or professional life is suffering, get the help you need. As the poet Rumi says, "It's rigged—everything, in your favor. So, there's nothing to worry about."

2. *Detach from the outcome.* We may not have control over every outcome, but we can change our relationship to it. If you cannot resolve a chronic situation in your life, hold true to an inner vision. Consider the para-Olympians who have lost a

limb but continue to live their dreams. They have reframed what it means to live a successful life.

3. ***Practice mindfulness.*** The practice of mindfulness awakens us to the presence of joy inherent in each moment. Each day try bringing your awareness to one task. If you are washing dishes, wash the dishes. Use your senses to enjoy the experience.

4. ***Share your gifts and talents.*** The challenges of life are opportunities to help you develop the spiritual qualities necessary to express your gifts. If someone had told me I'd have to transform myself to expand my writing, I would never have believed them, but it was true. Don't be afraid to share your passion with the world. If you cooperate with life, it'll bring out the best in you.

Safire Rose, M.A., J.D., is a poet, author, teacher of timeless wisdom, and interspiritual minister ordained by Agape International Spiritual Center and Centers for Spiritual Living. She is best known for her poem "She Let Go." Visit her website to learn about her upcoming book of poetry and free gift.

Safire-Rose.com

UNRAVELING
THE SECRETS OF
MONEY AND JOY

Kurt J. Rossi

Amid a sea of flashing red, white, and blue lights and the disarray of police sirens and radios, confusion overwhelmed me. Unable to grasp what was happening, I sought refuge in the darkness by closing my eyes.

My dad's face was the first I saw when I awoke. "You and your mom were in a bad car accident," he said.

I immediately asked, "Where is Mom?"

"She's in another room. She'll be okay," assured my dad.

Two days later, the doctor came in to check on my concussion. Holding up two fingers, he asked: "How many fingers am I holding up?"

I held up three. "How many fingers am I holding up?" I sarcastically replied.

He chuckled and signed my discharge papers.

I was seven years old.

Wrinkles on My Forehead

The accident my mom and I had been in turned into a court case. Not only did I have a concussion from the accident, but I also had a slight indentation on my forehead where I'd hit the seat in front of me.

So, it was pretty scary when the judge called me to the front of the courtroom so I could show him how my forehead wrinkled when I opened my eyes wide.

Later, I learned I would receive a five thousand-dollar settlement—a lot of money for a kid my age.

Little did I know that this fateful accident would catalyze my quest to unravel the secrets of money and joy.

Uncovering My Path

From a young age, I possessed a profound awareness and sensitivity to people's financial concerns, and my heart brimmed with compassion for those facing economic hardships. Consequently, as I pondered my career path during my college years, I found an irresistible pull toward finance.

I wasn't really interested in working in corporate finance; I wanted to help people feel more financially confident and make better choices with their money.

One evening, over dinner, Mom informed me: "Kurt, remember that settlement money? Well, you'll receive it in a few months, and it has grown to more than twenty-one thousand dollars."

Wow, I thought to myself, *the high-interest rate environment of the 1980s really compounded the growth of that settlement!*

The Stock Market Game

Many college students play The Stock Market Game™ without actual financial repercussions to gain practical experience using pretend money.

Since I was majoring in finance at college, my parents gave me total control over the settlement money I'd received. Boy, were they happy and relieved when I told them I'd invest it for my future rather than spend it all at once on a new Ford Mustang! However, I failed to anticipate that I would be immersed in the real stock market game, this time with real-life consequences, during one of the most overvalued markets in history—the dot-com bubble.

When the dot-com bubble burst, many investors sustained significant losses; unfortunately, I was no different—I lost nearly 50 percent of my investment value.

Ouch!

Besides learning how volatile markets can be, I also learned about one of the strongest emotions that money can trigger: fear.

The Number One Fear (It Isn't Death)

When I read this headline in *MarketWatch*, I got a sick, nervous feeling in the pit of my stomach: "Americans Are More Afraid of Running Out of Money Than Death."[14]

Wow! At first, the headline seemed more sensationalized hyperbole than truth. But when you consider that emotions around money extend far beyond just investing, some form of financial fear and worry is universal across all socioeconomic groups in the United States. No one is entirely immune from it. And very few seem to have a healthy relationship with their money. Instead, their relationship is often viewed through a lens of either prosperity or scarcity—and sometimes a little bit of both. My career would later teach me that fear was one of the myriad of feelings money can trigger in all of us.

Money as a Magnifier of Emotions

As I began my career, I moved from learning how people deal with money to seeing how they respond

---

4   Brett Arends, "Americans Are More Afraid Of Running Out of Money Than Death," *MarketWatch*, Dow Jones & Co., June 1, 2023, https://www.marketwatch.com/story/americans-are-more-afraid-of-running-out-money-than-death-ee5e22e9.

to it in action. For example, my client Claire—a strong, independent woman with a great sense of humor who valued planning for her future. She became an avid stock-market watcher, and when the markets went up, so did her happiness. And as her money grew, so did her appetite for more.

"Kurt, I want my money to grow even more!" she'd say with a twinkle in her eye.

"Okay," I replied, "where to now?"

She'd tell me, and we'd move the "goal post" further out. Then, I'd watch her happiness slump until she reached her new goal.

Claire was also a saver. But sadly, she passed away without ever spending her carefully curated money.

Watching her go through the roller coaster of happiness highs and lows, it suddenly hit me: When happiness is tied to money, it's short-lived.

Money is a magnifier of our emotions, intensifying the already existing feelings bubbling beneath the surface. And if we place money as the top priority in our lives, that means most of us are devoting a massive amount of energy chasing after more. Over the course of our lifetime, that's a lot of physical and emotional exertion!

Time, the Ultimate Currency

As I researched the relationship between money and happiness, I found that many studies affirmed what

I had long suspected—happiness plateaus beyond a certain income threshold.

Yet, I observed how people prioritize their lives around money, with some willing to give up almost anything to pursue more.

One day, I met John, a financially anxious entrepreneur. John remained uneasy despite dedicating an exhausting sixty hours a week to his business and amassing what American society deems the symbols of outward, material success (lots of money, a grand house, and a fleet of impressive cars).

So, I asked him a very pointed question: "John, if money didn't matter, what, if anything, would you do differently in your life today?"

John considered his answer and replied: "I would spend more time with family, especially with my children."

After crunching the numbers, I revealed: "John, you said that if money didn't matter, you'd spend more time with your family."

"Yes."

"Considering the savings you've accumulated and your financial projections, do you realize that you're exchanging valuable moments with your family today for leaving them more money in the future when you might not be around?"

"No, I hadn't thought of it that way before."

I nodded, waiting for him to process more.

"You're right. Time—not money—is the most valuable currency. I need to reassess my priorities in life."

The Game of Life

One evening, I walked past our living room and saw my children setting up the new board game they'd received from their grandparents—The Game of Life.[5]

My son was reading aloud from the instructions: "Hit the road for a roller coaster of adventure, family, unexpected surprises, and pets. The player with the most money at the end of the game wins."

Wait, I thought, *the player with the most money wins? There's something not quite right about that.* (Many of us in the United States have been raised with this approach to life. It's often ingrained in how we think about money and success.) *Maybe we need to reassess the rules for how we play.*

My Aha Moment

As I began to think about how life would change if we shifted our priorities, I came to a powerful realization: Clearing our attachment to money and re-prioritizing

---

5   The Game of Life: A Family Game, Milton Bradley, 1860.

our purpose allow us to reveal and explore the real treasures in life—joy, happiness, and peace.

Understanding how best to manage our money to alleviate this attachment and concern about money is essential. By crafting a holistic plan that addresses both immediate financial needs and future goals, we pave the way to a more mindful approach to our financial and overall well-being.

Ultimately, by diminishing the prominence of money in our lives, we liberate room for the truly joyful things—quality time with family, fostering friendships, engaging in volunteer work, or embarking on a journey of spiritual growth. These are the aspects that deserve our utmost priority and attention.

My Message to You

Throughout my career as a Certified Financial Planner and wealth advisor, I've focused on helping clients think less about money and more on discovering their joy.

My commitment has been to empower individuals to both accumulate wealth and discern authentic sources of contentment and fulfillment. I help them foster a mindset that allows them to break free from the perpetual worry about finances and, instead, immerse themselves in the richness of life.

I encourage you to embark on your own financial journey. What are the secrets of money and joy for you?

Take a moment to contemplate that question. And when you go inward to find your answers, you might just find that true wealth lies in embracing what brings you lasting joy.

 **Kurt Rossi**, LPL Financial Member FINRA/SIPC, is a Certified Financial Planner and the owner of Independent Wealth Management, a financial planning team dedicated to helping people uncover the meaning of true wealth in their lives. He enjoys life with his family and spending time in nature, especially the ocean.

IndependentWM.com

JUST SURVIVING ISN'T ENOUGH: TAKING BACK YOUR CAREER

Benjamin Sims

Imagine being trapped in a workplace where you are constantly on edge, where you fear the next explosive outburst from your boss, and where you're never sure if your hard work will be acknowledged or undermined. This is the reality many employees face when dealing with toxic bosses. The workplace becomes a battlefield of manipulation, where employees are pitted against one another and trust is a scarce commodity.

A toxic boss often wields fear as their weapon of choice. They use it to control and manipulate employees, pushing them to comply with their demands through threats, guilt, or intimidation. It's a soul-sucking experience, with employees feeling trapped in a never-ending cycle of fear and uncertainty.

My Personal Journey: Navigating a Toxic Workplace

I recall a time in my career when I had to navigate this treacherous terrain. I was tasked with completing a project, and my boss constantly changed the project's objectives and requirements, leaving me in a perpetual state of confusion. One moment, I would be praised for my work, and the next, I would be criticized and told to start over. It felt like I was walking on eggshells, never knowing what mood my boss would be in and how it would impact my work.

But one day, as I filled out the annual employee engagement survey, I had a moment of reflection. I had two options: to be open and honest, or to provide positive feedback to protect my own interests. I chose the latter, hoping it would make the organization more attractive, thereby attracting employees who could help change the culture. Yet this turned out to be a futile effort.

During my performance review, my boss accused me of trying to sabotage the survey results and dismissed the survey as an inappropriate platform to voice concerns. Instead, I was told to address any issues directly with my boss—the very source of my "survival mentality." In that moment, I realized I was not alone. Two other colleagues had rated their experiences similarly. I knew it was time to build a coalition to confront this toxic behavior.

A toxic boss's manipulation can also extend to creating a culture of favoritism, where certain employees receive preferential treatment while others are left to fend for themselves. This divisive behavior fosters an environment where employees are in constant competition for their boss's approval, creating a toxic and unhealthy workplace.

The Impact of a Toxic Workplace

The final straw occurred during my one-on-one. I had pumped myself up to prepare for this one-on-one Teams call. At 2:00 p.m., it was time to log on. My anxiety level was off the charts, and I had used all the techniques learned in our wellness calls. I couldn't have ever prepared myself for what I was about to encounter.

I joined the call, and I started by talking through the major projects currently on my plate. Then my boss asked me: "What do you do?" I immediately felt myself getting defensive, followed by feeling completely deflated and devalued. I knew I could no longer work for this leader.

The toll of working in a toxic workplace extends far beyond the office walls. It takes a significant mental and emotional toll on employees, leading to a range of negative consequences. The constant stress and anxiety of such an environment can result in depression, burnout, and various mental health issues.

One of the most significant impacts of a toxic workplace is the erosion of employees' confidence and self-esteem. When subjected to relentless criticism, negative feedback, and blame from their boss, employees often lose their sense of self-worth. This erosion of self-esteem seeps into their personal lives, causing dissatisfaction and unhappiness in other areas.

The impact of a toxic workplace is extensive and detrimental to employees' mental, emotional, and physical well-being. Recognizing the signs of a toxic workplace is vital for one's health and happiness. By identifying these signs, employees can take action to address the situation before it consumes them.

Taking Ownership of Your Career

A poignant lesson can be drawn from the story of a boss who used their power to negatively impact an employee's career path without explanation or improvement opportunity. It highlights the importance of taking ownership of your career and not relying solely on your boss or organization to dictate your path. While bosses may have the power to influence your career trajectory, you ultimately hold the reins of your own success.

I had a choice: to endure the negative impact of my boss's actions in the hopes of a better future or proactively seek new opportunities that would recognize my worth. The choice to "take back your career" and seek a new path in a different organization is a powerful reminder that sometimes surviving isn't enough.

Steve Jobs' famous quote resonates with this sentiment: "Your work is going to fill a large part of your life, and the only way to be truly satisfied is to do what you believe is great work. And the only way to do great work is to love what you do. If you haven't found it yet, keep looking. Don't settle." This quote underscores the importance of seeking fulfilling work that aligns with your values and goals, even if it requires taking risks.

Taking Action

Here are a few practical steps to break free from a toxic workplace and reclaim your confidence:

1. **Engage in Self-Reflection and Assessment.**
   - Evaluate the situation. Take an honest look at your workplace and determine if it's genuinely toxic. Document specific incidents, behaviors, or patterns that contribute to the toxicity.

2. **Seek Support.**
   - Talk to trusted colleagues or friends. Share your experiences and feelings with people you trust to gain emotional support and perspective.
   - Consider therapy or counseling. A mental health professional can help you cope with the emotional toll of a toxic workplace and provide guidance.

3. **Set Boundaries.**
   - Define your limits and communicate them with toxic coworkers or supervisors. Be assertive but professional.

4. **Document Everything.**
   - Document instances of toxic behavior, including dates, times, people involved, and any evidence you can gather (emails, messages, etc.).

5. **Explore Internal Opportunities.**
   - If you want to stay with your current employer, consider transferring to a different department or team where the work environment may be healthier.

6. **Network and Update Your Resume.**
   - Attend industry events, connect on LinkedIn, and seek out potential job opportunities.
   - Make sure your resumê and LinkedIn profile reflect your skills and experiences.

7. **Focus on Your Health and Well-Being:**
   - Maintain a healthy lifestyle, get enough sleep, exercise regularly, and practice stress-reduction techniques like meditation or yoga.

8. **Exit Gracefully.**
   - When you secure a new job, resign from your toxic workplace professionally. Give the proper notice and finish your remaining tasks to maintain your reputation.

9. **Rebuild Your Confidence.**
   - Understand that leaving a toxic environment is a significant achievement.
   - Focus on your strengths and achievements. Celebrate your successes.

- Surround yourself with supportive people who uplift your confidence.
- Consider working with a career coach or therapist to rebuild your self-esteem.

Taking these steps will help you recognize that you have the agency to shape your career and take control of your professional life.

Moving Forward

Moving forward after a toxic workplace experience can be challenging, but it's crucial to focus on the future and use the lessons learned to build a better work environment. Here are some steps to help you move forward:

- Be kind to yourself and acknowledge the strength it took to leave a toxic workplace.
- Understand that healing and recovery take time, and it's okay to seek support from professionals or support groups.
- Define clear career goals and aspirations for your future.
- Use your past experiences to inform your decisions and ensure you choose a healthier work environment.

- Cultivate relationships with colleagues who share your values and promote a positive workplace culture.
- Seek out mentors or advisors who can provide guidance and encouragement.
- Continue prioritizing self-care to maintain your mental and emotional well-being.
- Focus on activities that bring you joy and fulfillment outside of work.
- If you decide to start a new job, actively contribute to creating a positive and supportive workplace culture.
- Advocate for transparent communication, empathy, and fairness.

Moving forward after a toxic workplace experience requires effort and self-compassion. Remember Maya Angelou's words: "I can be changed by what happens to me, but I refuse to be reduced by it." You have the capacity to overcome challenges and emerge stronger. Use the lessons learned to take action, seek support, set goals, practice self-care, and create a positive work environment.

By applying the knowledge gained, you can take control of your professional life and create a positive and fulfilling work environment that values and appreciates your contributions.

Benjamin Sims is a visionary HR leader shaping tomorrow's workforce using a dynamic, solution-oriented approach with innovative strategies that invigorate organizations, propelling them toward unprecedented growth and effectiveness. Benjamin is not just an inspiring leader but also a tireless advocate for employee engagement and a passionate contributor to the community.

linkedin.com/in/benjamin-s-91940516

RUNNING AWAY

Susan Sisk

When I was four years old, I ran away. My friend and I were outside playing with a bucket of mud, each of us stirring it with our sticks. When it was the perfect texture, we used our sticks to throw it against the side of the house next to us, watching it hit with a satisfying *thwap* as it stuck to the siding. We were having a glorious time until the owner of the house realized what we were doing and started shouting wildly at us for creating a mess on the side of her house. I remember feeling panic and dread, and not knowing what to do, I started running down the sidewalk, away from the screaming neighbor. I ran until my legs gave out and I tripped and fell.

Sitting on the sidewalk with skinned knees, I started to cry. I was lost, and I felt so alone. Fear and helplessness consumed me until someone saw me sitting there crying and stayed with me until my mother raced home from work in a terrified frenzy. She went door-to-door throughout the neighborhood until she found me crying on the sidewalk with a strange man sitting next to me.

I think about that little girl, and I wonder, *What made her run instead of staying to face the fear she felt?* And then I wonder, *Are there areas in my life where I am still running away instead of standing still and facing whatever emotions I don't want to feel?*

People often say, "Cheer up!" or "Don't worry!" rather than tell us it's OK to feel whatever you are feeling and sit with that emotion until it transmutes into something else. As parents, we comfort our children when they are dysregulated and try to find ways to make them happy again, rather than helping them acknowledge that it's OK to feel whatever they are feeling. Suppressing negative emotions is often associated with strength and health, while expressing them is often equated with weakness.

While striving to avoid emotions may bring some short-term relief, it doesn't really work long-term. The resistance we are feeling takes up much of our attention and energy, while the core issues remain. Many try to numb their emotions through drugs, alcohol, or media-binging.

I spent six years in a job feeling completely and utterly miserable. The environment was toxic, and the head of the company (to whom I reported) struggled with leadership skills. His method of communicating with top leadership was saying negative things about us to our colleagues, hoping it would get back to us and we would make changes accordingly. All of us knew that the boss was disparaging each one of us behind our backs, yet he would never say anything to us directly.

I stayed with the company because I thought I could make a difference; I told myself I could stick it out, even though the constant negativity and stress was making me physically sick. My way of numbing was through food and binge-watching TV—I didn't have the energy to exercise. I developed an autoimmune disease and gained twenty-five pounds. I felt awful about myself physically on top of how miserable I was mentally. I was exhausted and just wanted to sleep—looking back, I'm sure I was suffering from depression.

Just when I thought I couldn't take it any longer, the company chose to make some leadership changes, and to my complete relief, I was on the list. That day was one of the happiest of my life, and the glee I felt can hardly be described.

But when I broke the good news to my husband and my friends, they were shocked. They had no idea how miserable and unhappy I had been and hadn't realized the extent of the physical issues I was having. I realized I had never revealed my feelings about working at this company; instead, I had always led everyone to believe that all was well!

Hmm. Did I not tell anyone the truth because I didn't want to make them feel uncomfortable, or did I not allow myself to truly feel all the negative emotions I was feeling? The fact that I was physically sick is a good indicator that my body was feeling the negative emotions I had not allowed myself to acknowledge.

Just like that little four-year-old girl, I was running away. Instead of standing up and taking responsibility for my emotions and facing what I was feeling, I turned and ran.

That realization was a turning point for me. After acknowledging that I had not been truthful with my feelings to family and friends and realizing how sick I had become physically, I made a vow to change. But how?

Emotions are simply energy that is felt in the body, hence the name *feelings*—we feel them physically. This is a new concept for many people (it was for me!) who spend much of their time focused on their thoughts instead of how they feel. A felt emotion in the body can be translated into an actual physical pain or sensation, or perhaps just as some pressure or tension. Think about the times you get nervous and feel "butterflies" in your stomach, or after a particularly stressful day, you develop a headache. Or when you imagine something you're worried about, you feel a "knot" in your stomach. I realized that the "heavy" feelings in my stomach and chest that I felt every

Sunday night when I thought about going to work on Monday were a direct result of the anxiety and dread I had about my toxic boss.

I spent a lot of time researching and learning about emotions. I learned that feeling emotions is not about controlling them but rather giving up control and learning to trust. By recognizing my emotions and allowing myself to acknowledge and breathe through them, they would diminish or dissolve altogether. This didn't necessarily mean that the core issue had gone away, but it did allow me to face it from a much calmer and rational perspective.

It took a while for me to become aware of when I was thinking versus feeling, but it has become easier over time. I developed a practice of starting my day with meditation each morning, and as part of my practice, I intentionally check in with my body to see if I notice any sensations or tension. If I do, I acknowledge them and breathe through them. I ask myself what the core issue is and then visualize myself dealing with the issue in a calm, kind, compassionate way. This allows me to stay in my power rather than feeling like the issue has control over me.

I recently started a new job, where the culture is collaborative, the people I work with are eager to help, and the office I report to is supportive and honest. I'm back to caring for myself with a healthy diet and exercising, my weight has returned to normal, and my energy levels are back where they should be.

I've added another practice to my morning meditation by asking myself if there are any areas of my life where I am holding back my emotions and not playing full-out. Am I avoiding standing up and facing something because it's too difficult? Am I running away again, like that four-year-old girl? I have found that, without exception, facing difficult situations and feelings head on ALWAYS has a better outcome than denying my feelings. It has made my relationships deeper, my work more meaningful, and my health more vibrant.

Even though the six years I spent working for a toxic company were miserable, I am grateful for them as the experience led me to a major realization that truly changed my life.

The day I was writing this chapter, the following message popped up on my social media:

I think there is pressure on people to turn every negative into a positive, but we should be allowed to say, "I went through something really strange and awful, and it has altered me forever." (Marian Keyes)

I couldn't agree more.

Susan Sisk is a finance executive and transformational life coach. Her superpowers include making deep connections with others and helping them to live an authentic life. A lifelong learner, she has numerous certifications in coaching and other transformational tools. Susan loves to play pickleball with her husband and spend time with her family—especially her grandchildren!

CHEERLEADER, SORORITY PRESIDENT, AND ANXIETY . . . OH MY!

E. Denise Sutter

Throughout my life, anxiety has been my constant companion.

But here's the crazy thing: I was a cheerleader in high school. And in college, I was president of the Chi Omega sorority at Oglethorpe University in Atlanta, Georgia. For someone grappling with anxiety, these are front-and-center leadership positions seemingly impossible to maintain.

How did I manage them?

As a youth, I experienced the typical nerves and shyness associated with social anxiety that most teens feel when meeting new people and speaking in front of groups. Yet, lurking beneath that was something more.

While no teenager enjoys being judged or embarrassed in front of their peers, the anxiety that squatted within me was far more serious—a fear that could and eventually would significantly impact my life.

Always the Quiet One

I've always been a quiet person. Even as a cheerleader. I know that doesn't sound like the typical personality profile for a cheerleader, made even stranger when I was awarded the "most school spirit" my senior year.

What?

Yes, true!

Even through college, when I was a Chi Omega officer, I was quiet. I didn't like being in the spotlight and was a reluctant leader. Yet, I would and could lead. But I really didn't want to!

(I know. It doesn't make sense. Keep reading—it will!)

As I aged, my anxiety increased. And in college, it was on the verge of surfacing. To tamp it down, I began using alcohol. Beer was my drink of choice. Most college students drink to have fun, loosen up, and party. I was drinking to squash my anxiety, which, as anyone who suffers from anxiety knows, did the opposite—it heightened it!

The Only Way It Worked

I was raised in a family that instilled in me the values of doing my best and succeeding at what I did, no matter the cost. I was told to "push through it" when facing challenges and "suck it up" when times got tough.

So, the way I coped with my mounting anxiety was to step into a role. If I was playing the role of cheerleader or sorority president, I could function. In the same way an actor assumes the persona of their role, so did I. I became a cheerleader and radiated school spirit because that's what cheerleaders do. I stepped into Chi Omega officer roles and got things done because it was what leaders are expected to do.

I pushed through and sucked it up. That was the only way I could perform in front of crowds, mingle with diverse groups of people, and interact in social situations. Yet anxiety threatened to close in on me the minute I stepped out of the role.

My First Panic Attack

With all that mounting anxiety, it might be hard for you to believe that it wasn't until I turned thirty-three that I had my first panic attack. Nearly *two decades* had passed before my anxiety erupted and gripped me with an iron fist. I thought I was having a heart attack!

- Chest pains . . . check.
- Pounding and racing heart . . . undeniably! My heart was practically doing a marathon in my chest.

- Feeling lightheaded . . . yep. I felt like I might faint any second.
- Overwhelmed with the feeling of impending doom . . . definitely! The dread was suffocating.

These were all classic signs associated with having a heart attack. So, you can imagine my bafflement when the emergency room doctor told me: "Denise, your heart is fine."

"What?" I blurted out in disbelief.

"Your test results indicate you haven't experienced a cardiac event."

That's not possible! I thought, my mind racing with confusion. "Well, then, what's going on?"

The doctor met my gaze and said calmly, "You're having a panic attack."

I was dumbfounded. How could this be? I'd weathered the storm of almost losing my mom to cancer, the heartbreaking experience of leaving Alex, my newborn daughter, in the neonatal intensive care unit for three agonizing weeks, the turmoil of a gut-wrenching divorce, and the challenges of parenting as a single mom for four long years. All these anxiety-inducing events and I was just now having my first panic attack?

On top of that, life was good! I'd met the love of my life, Scott. We were about to be married, and Alex and I were preparing to start a fresh chapter with him in sunny California. Everything was falling into place.

So, why was I having a panic attack now?

A House of Cards

The long and short of it is that anxiety doesn't just happen. It creeps up on you, similar to how a house of cards is built one card upon another.

In its early stages, anxiety might present with subtle physical and emotional symptoms (social anxiety) that go unnoticed or are attributed to other causes (nerves and shyness), making it difficult to identify until it becomes more pronounced.

Like the foundation of a house, anxiety begins with a trigger that doesn't get addressed. This foundational stressor then becomes the card that supports the entire structure.

As life goes on, more cards are added. I learned to cope with the anxiety by stepping into roles and using alcohol to numb myself.

Some cards might be slightly crooked or unstable, representing unresolved emotional or physical traumas that haven't been addressed. Almost losing my mom to cancer and going through a divorce were two of mine. These cards may not seem like a big deal initially, but they add to the overall instability.

Major life transitions—even happy ones—are like adding a handful of cards all at once. These transitions require us to adjust and adapt. And without a strong foundation, the entire structure will wobble.

Some people, like me, have an inherited predisposition to anxiety. My parents exhibited anxiety, as did my grandparents, and their generational way of coping with it was to establish rules of conduct. Their rules imprinted on me the importance of doing my best and succeeding at what I did, no matter the cost—"push through it" and "suck it up."

As more cards are added to the house of anxiety, it will eventually collapse. That's why it took twenty years for my first panic attack to topple me.

If this has happened to you, you're not alone. According to the Anxiety and Depression Association of America: Anxiety disorders are the most common mental illness in the U.S., affecting 40 million adults each year.[6] And according to statistics published by the World Health Organization: In 2019, 301 million people were living with an anxiety disorder, including 58 million children and adolescents.[7]

6 "Anxiety Disorders – Facts and Statistics," Anxiety and Depression Association of America, accessed October 3, 2023, https://adaa.org/understanding-anxiety/facts-statistics.

7 "Mental Disorders," World Health Organization, accessed October 3, 2023, https://www.who.int/news-room/fact-sheets/detail/mental-disorders.

My Message of Hope

The message of hope I offer is this:

- Within you lies the pathway to inner peace and boundless freedom. Debilitating anxiety need not be your lifelong companion, and you need not be enslaved by the fear of panic attacks.
- Embrace anxiety as a part of your life but refuse to let it dictate the terms of your life.
- Step boldly into the knowledge that you possess the strength to master it. Trust unequivocally in your innate capacity to nurture and heal yourself.

Here are three things that helped and continue to help me deal with my anxiety. I hope they will help you, too. They are:

1. *Establish boundaries.* Boundaries are your compass in the turbulent sea of anxiety and your shield against the chaos of panic. Say no when something doesn't resonate with you. Learn to distinguish between personal growth's discomfort and panic's suffocating grip. Set these boundaries for yourself and communicate them to others.

2. *Forgive and accept yourself.* I know this is a hard thing to do. In the depths of anxiety-induced fear, I've made countless mistakes. I've made poor decisions, overindulged in self-destructive habits, and lashed out at those I loved because I was in pain.

3. *Face your past, acknowledge your mistakes, make amends where possible, and seek forgiveness when necessary.* Most importantly, extend grace to yourself as you journey onward.

4. *Embrace the power of hope.* Let hope float and be your guiding star. Believe with unwavering certainty that healing and growth are possible. Trust in the flow of life, take it one day at a time, and step forward with unshakable faith. Know that things can and will get better.

By embracing the power of hope, you signal to the universe your intention and willingness to surrender to the flow and go with it, not against it. Welcome each day for the opportunity for restoration and transformation it brings.

You are a resilient person with an infinite capacity for renewal. You will heal. You will thrive. And you will emerge triumphant from the shadow of anxiety. I believe in you. Go.

E. Denise Sutter, an energetic artist and intuitive healer, thrives with her husband, Scott, her grown children, Alex, Max, Jackson, Nicky, and her beloved grandson, Daniel. Her battle with anxiety fuels her passion for sharing hope through her art and story, inspiring others to find the courage to heal and grow.

ElaineDeniseSutter.com

THE ALCHEMY
OF
TRANSFORMATION
AND TRUST
Nancy Turner

The sun hung low in the sky on a late winter afternoon, casting a warm, golden hue across the room where I sat sewing buttons on my wedding dress. A few days before, I had graduated from the University of Wisconsin, and tomorrow was the big day.

Not only was leaving school behind a significant change, but I was embarking on an even bigger transition. I was nervously asking that niggling question all soon-to-be brides ask: *Am I ready for this?*

Yet, deep down inside, I knew that marrying my high school sweetheart and moving cross-country was the right thing to do. I knew that saying "I do" wasn't just about getting married; it was saying "yes" to what would be the portal to a new life, one that would take me from the familiar streets of my hometown in Wisconsin to the sunny shores of California.

Even years later, after I'd divorced, I still knew I married the right person at the right time.

Bold, Fearless Spirit

Growing up, I'd possessed an innate trust in my intuition. I was a bold, fearless spirit and could take that leap of faith because I trusted that if I fell, there would be a safety net to catch me.

Looking back, I know now that it often looked to others as if I were taking a risk or, at the very least, I hadn't thought things through. But that wasn't the case. I knew intuitively that what I was doing was right for me.

I could be bold and fearless because I knew life to be a series of choices, and I believed that if I followed my inner guidance and took purposeful steps along the path, I'd get to where I was supposed to be.

Trust and Step

Remember that scene in *Indiana Jones and the Last Crusade* where Indy must cross an invisible bridge to get to the Holy Grail?[8] With his father close to death and the Grail the only hope to save him, Indy rushes

---

8   "Leap of Faith," *Indian Jones and the Last Crusade,* directed by Steven Spielberg (1989, Hollywood, CA: Paramount Pictures).

through a doorway below a carved lion's head and finds himself standing on the edge of a cliff.

On the opposite side is a doorway . . . in between a chasm. With no other options, Indy steps into thin air. And as every movie watcher held their breath, his foot hit solid ground.

That's how it was with me. I've trusted that the support I needed would be there and the next step would appear. I didn't need to have everything mapped out for me to take the next step.

Intuitive Guidance System

Years later, my current husband and I were considering a move to the Pacific Northwest. We wanted to live either in Washington or Oregon, and we decided that whoever got a job first, that's where we'd move.

At this point, I was working at Bank of America in San Francisco. My boss approached me and said: "Nancy, I'd like to offer you a role on our Executive and Leadership Succession Planning Team.

Oh-oh.

"Nick, thank you for this wonderful opportunity. However, Bob and I are planning on moving to the Pacific Northwest soon, so, it wouldn't be fair to accept your offer."

"When will you be moving?"

"We don't know."

"Well, then, work for me in this new position until you do."

So I did. And as it turned out, a year later Nick was instrumental in helping me get a promotion to Bank of America in Oregon. Yes, Oregon. In the Pacific Northwest!

I've always trusted my intuitive guidance system to decide what inner-inspired actions to take. Here's how you can do it too:

- Visualize the future you want.
- Put it out into the universe.
- Trust it will manifest.
- Let it go.
- Remain open to what comes.
- Be eager for change.

That's the alchemy of transformation.

Bold, Trusting Move

Five years later, I trusted my intuitive guidance system again and left Bank of America—this time to start up my own business.

By this time, I'd been working at Bank of America for twenty years. I liked what I did and could have contentedly stayed there for the rest of my career. But the universe had other plans.

As part of my job, I worked with entrepreneurs who were doing interesting things with their businesses. And, over time, I began to feel the inner tug to start up a business of my own.

When? I asked my inner knower.

Now, it nudged.

I put the idea "out there" and trusted it would manifest. I let it go while remaining open and eager for change. I knew that as nudges and opportunities appeared, I could tap into my inner knowing to decide what actions to take.

True to form, I trusted the voice within, left my job, and started The Turner Group, where I began my own interesting work with leaders committed to creating inspiring, engaging, and thriving work environments.

Opportunity Knocks

All was going well until the summer of 2004 when one of my big projects was "unexpectedly" delayed. There was nothing for me to do but wait. And then, with time on my hands, I began hearing—from three different sources—about a job at Nike that would be perfect for me.

So, I took that as a sign from the universe, and before I knew it, I put my business on hold and joined Nike.

After working at Nike for fifteen years, once again I felt that inner tug to leave the corporate world and return to my business. As it turns out, the time I spent at Nike was exactly what I needed to take my business to the next level.

Amazing things happen when you allow the universe to illuminate your path:

- Doors, once closed, miraculously open.
- Opportunities land, seemingly out of the blue, at your feet.
- Things you thought impossible to do, be, or have naturally occur.

Today, I call myself Chief Leadership Alchemist at The Turner Group. I work with leaders to create magical transformation in their lives. And I love what I do!

Alchemy of Transformation

In its broader sense, the alchemy of transformation refers to the personal and spiritual transformation that occurs when you undergo a significant change in your thoughts, beliefs, or behaviors.

Much like the alchemy of old that aimed to transform base metals into noble metals such as gold, today's alchemy is a metaphor for personal growth and inner transformation. It signifies inner change and development that leads to higher states of awareness and understanding.

Instead of turning lead into gold, today's alchemy transmutes your "base" qualities (like fear and shame) into "noble" qualities (like wisdom and love) through a process of inner trust combined with aligned outer action.

It's not about taking a risk or trusting blindly.

It's about making choices that feel right—ones that resonate with your inner wisdom—all while grounding yourself in the present moment. When you don't listen to this inner wisdom and guidance, you will remain stuck in the base qualities of fear and shame—resulting in lead, not gold.

So, as you visualize the future, trust it to manifest, even if it does so in unexpected ways and surprising timing.

Let go of the fear and worry.

Open to the magical, alchemical process that turns everything into gold.

Nuggets of Inspiration

As I finish this chapter, I leave you with these three nuggets of inspiration:

1. **You are not alone.** Even when it seems like solitude is your only companion, remember

that there exists a multitude of beings, both visible and hidden, who are working harmoniously for your ultimate well-being and greatest good.

2. **You co-create your life.** Your life is not solely of your making; you co-create it with numerous entities. Beyond the individuals currently walking beside you, your inner self, higher self, the universe, and other cosmic forces perpetually envelop you, eager and prepared to aid in the manifestation of your deepest desires.

3. **You have the power to shape your future.** You can trust your intuition. It communicates from within through gentle nudges and tugs, a profound sense of knowing, and a feeling of alignment. The more you pay attention to it, the stronger it grows.

So, muster your courage and step out in faith, knowing that a path will appear before you and a safety net will appear below with each step you take.

My story is a testament to the alchemy of transformation and trust. Face your own challenges with an open heart and abiding trust in the magic of change.

Trust in the alchemy of transformation.

Nancy Turner, a seasoned consultant and leadership coach, has trusted her intuition as well as knowledge and experience while navigating Fortune 500 giants and honing her instincts through life's twists. With wisdom from her journey, she guides leaders on their own life transitions. From the heartland of Wisconsin to the captivating Oregon Coast, Nancy's story inspires.

NancyTurner.com

PHOENIX RISING
OUT OF THE
ASHES OF
CO-DEPENDENCY

Gina Urzi

It wasn't a surprise I ended up marrying a man who struggled with alcohol and drug addiction. Given my upbringing, it felt like the natural course of things. Many women in my life carried the self-imposed responsibility of caregiving for a partner with substance abuse issues.

I met Nathan in college. I was a cheerleader, and he played football. We bumped into each other at an athletic booster dinner when we were sophomores, and after our first date, we knew we had a connection. Despite meeting in college, we discovered we had lived just five miles apart growing up and even had mutual friends.

Footloose and Fancy-Free

One year earlier, my previous boyfriend and I had broken up. I know it was because I was smothering him with my caregiving and always trying to change him. Back then, I thought that's what I was supposed to do—"mom" your man.

When Nathan entered the picture, I was living at home, going to school, and working three jobs.

I was single, happy, having fun with my girlfriends, and thoroughly enjoying my life. I relished my newfound freedom. I took care of no one except myself. Love, and certainly a committed relationship, was the furthest thing from my mind.

Yet, nature knew better.

Nature Abhors a Vacuum

Nature doesn't tolerate empty spaces; something always rushes in to fill the void.

That was Nathan. He stepped in to fill my caregiving void.

At that time, I wasn't aware that my role as a caregiver was actually a form of co-dependent behavior. I also didn't realize Nathan came from a co-dependent family, which made it all too easy for us to begin our dance of co-dependency. I quickly slid into the "mom" role that was familiar to both of us.

Vacuum filled. All was well in my world.

Except it really wasn't.

Wedded Bliss or Amiss?

In 1997, we tied the knot and relocated to Florida. That's when I began to sense something was looming.

At first, it was a little thing, here and there. Then I started noticing a troubling pattern—Nathan was lying about the frequency of his drinking and marijuana use.

With my co-dependent tendencies, I unwittingly became the caretaking hero, determined to rescue the situation. I was the designated driver when he overindulged. I made excuses for his behavior and justified his actions to others and myself.

The real issue was that I had my blinders on, and I was committed to picking up the pieces—anything to make the immediate problem disappear and the pain go away. After all, what wife wants to admit that she married a substance-abusing alcoholic? My job was to fix it. Not confront it.

Until I couldn't.

Trying to Hold My Marital World Together

Nathan drank in college and smoked pot, but everyone did—see, I was making excuses for him even then. However, after we married, his drinking and smoking escalated, and then a series of injuries created a gateway to a new addiction: Vicodin. While stashing bags of pot under the stairs and in cabinets in the garage and lying about the number of drinks he was consuming, he was also popping pills like candy.

Then, in 2003, Alex was born. We were thrilled to welcome her into our family, making heartfelt promises to be the best parents ever! Nathan vowed to cut down on his drinking and drug usage, and with blinders firmly in place, I believed him.

Silly me. He just got better at sneaking and hiding.

Then, Nathan got a promotion at work. I was thirty-eight weeks pregnant with our second child, and because Alex came early, I knew this baby could arrive at any time.

"Honey, if you decide to celebrate, please come home early, just in case," I requested.

He agreed, but at 3:00 a.m., he walked through the door after a long night of partying.

At 5:00 a.m., I went into labor.

The contractions were so intense I couldn't possibly drive. So, we bundled up our toddler, Alex, and Nathan took the wheel as we sped toward the hospital. There were a lot of cars on the freeway. Nathan was intoxicated, stressed, and weaving through traffic. I was screaming through my contractions and bracing against the dashboard as Nathan sped down the shoulder of the road.

It's a miracle we made it in one piece.

Nathan's parents were waiting for us at the hospital. And as we handed Alex over to their care, I overheard his father exclaim: "Holy smokes, it smells like a distillery in here!"

Not now!

Although Nathan was present for the birth of our son, Ben, he soon left to "sleep off" his hangover and didn't return until the following day. The sad truth was I knew that he wouldn't come back to check on us.

My family was complete, and I had never felt so alone.

Marital House on Fire

Tension was building between us; our fighting grew, he partied more, and I continued covering for him.

My marital house was on fire, and I was watching it burn to the ground with no way to extinguish it. The dance of co-dependency that had defined our relationship was no longer sustainable. The deeply ingrained beliefs I had carried with me from my upbringing, which had defined my understanding of being a "good" wife, no longer aligned with my reality.

I was ready to get help.

A good coach is worth their weight in gold, and I discovered that when I met Grace. Although I'd been in therapy before, nothing clicked until I started seeing a Conscious Leadership coach in 2013.

Grace was the perfect coach for me. She was grounded, funny, and nonjudgmental. Coaching with her applied the pressure I needed to wake up and see what I was or wasn't doing. To stop complaining, accept responsibility, and change.

Like all things lasting, the changes I needed to make took time—three years. Thus, I was well prepared when I was ready to confront these two truths:

- I had been attempting to control my marriage from a place of fear.
- Each time I blamed Nathan for our circumstances, I was victimizing myself.

At the time, I was forty-one, with a fourteen-year-old daughter and an eleven-year-old son.

Now what? I asked myself.

The answer came two years later in the form of a watershed moment when Nathan overdosed in front of me and our children.

He was taking up to forty-five Vicodin a day, and a batch he had bought was laced with fentanyl. If you've never seen someone overdose, it's a highly traumatic event. Your emotions range from fear and shock to anger and guilt. I felt them all.

Our neighbor was a physician who ran over immediately to attend to Nathan. But by that time, he was coherent enough to rationalize the overdose.

All that remained were ashes.

Phoenix Rising

There's no turning back when you realize the truth about your situation. Two years later, I found the courage to sit Nathan down and say: "I don't want to continue like this. I want a partner who wants to be with me and work together on our relationship."

And you know what he said?

"I know. Neither do I. I was waiting until the kids went to college."

Imagine that!

While my Phoenix had been rising from the ashes, his bird had already flown the coop.

I had to reconcile with my fear and *perceived* control of situations. It was an illusion. I couldn't change, motivate, or save anyone. As hard as I tried, as deeply as I loved, it didn't make a difference.

In "trying" so hard, I had lost myself. My work was to heal my patterns, forgive, and love myself for not having the awareness or tools until I did.

Today, a decade later, I'm in a much different space.

I own my own home and business.

I'm a single mom supporting my college-age children, surrounded by family and friends. I travel the United States teaching Conscious Leadership to people, teams, and organizations. And I'm genuinely happy—for the first time. Nathan is also. He is clean, married, a great dad, and a good friend.

What I went through brought me to where I am today. And along my journey, I've discovered this life truth: It all comes down to awareness, acceptance, and choice.

- Awareness that everything happening to us is happening *for* us
- Lovingly accepting and forgiving ourselves
- Knowing we have a choice, even when it seems we don't

To this day, I continue a practice I began when my Phoenix was arising from the ashes that may be helpful to you, too. Upon awakening, I ask myself: What do I choose today? Then, I go inward, become still, and listen for the answer.

It is a profoundly simple question that always guides me in the right direction. And it's available anytime.

Now it's your turn.

What will you choose today?

Gina Urzi, CEO of True Aim Coaching, draws on her Phoenix-rising journey to ignite hope and facilitate growth in individuals, teams, and companies. She cultivates strong work cultures and high-performing teams deeply connected in trust. Beyond her transformative work, Gina enjoys time with her two children and being in nature.

TrueAimCoaching.com

ANGELS WATCHING OVER ME

Alyssa DiDomenico

Now I lay me down to sleep,
I pray the Lord my soul to keep.
If I should die before I wake . . .

"No. Not on my watch!"

Wait! What?

And then I felt the loving light of God wrap me in warmth.

Although this was the first time God spoke to me, it wasn't the last.

And not only God.

December 17, 2009

I was eighteen.

We were living in New Jersey; surgery was scheduled for 9:00 a.m. The temperature was hovering right above freezing, and it was partly sunny outside.

I was wearing a sweatshirt and pants, and my beloved Build-a-Bear Christmas reindeer that I had made for the occasion was tucked protectively underneath my arm. With Mom and Dad by my side, we drove to the hospital.

It's amazing how crystal-clear memories are when significant events happen.

A Few Months Before

I'd been in the pool with my friends, having fun. I dove off the board and into the water when suddenly, I felt blebs popping in my lungs.

Ouch!

Blebs are air-filled cysts trapped between the chest wall and the lungs. When they rupture, the air held in the blebs escapes into the chest cavity, leading to a partial or complete collapse of the lungs.

People can live their whole life with blebs and never know it.

Not me.

Living with Blebs

I'd been having blebs for a while. The first time took me by surprise. It was the year before, between recovering from pneumonia and my first back surgery. I had just executed an Olympic-worthy back two-and-a-half somersault dive (just kidding) into the pool when blebs started rupturing, and my right lung collapsed.

Wow, did that hurt!

Into the hospital I went.

Then, one year later, it happened again. This time, my left lung collapsed.

Oh goodie. Another hospital visit!

My lungs used to rupture only when I was jumping around or diving off the board. Now, they began happening randomly!

This was a real problem because I had just started college, and I never knew when they were going to rupture.

So, in October, my parents took me to a pulmonologist who scheduled me for surgery at Nemours Children's Hospital in Wilmington, Delaware.

Working around my school schedule, December 17, 2009, was my date with God.

Here's the Head Scratcher

The pulmonologist couldn't figure out why I was having blebs because I didn't fit the standard profile:

- I wasn't a man.
- I didn't smoke.

- I didn't have emphysema or tuberculosis.
- Although I had asthma as a kid, it only occurred when I had an upper respiratory infection. And I quickly grew out of that.
- I wasn't a scuba diver—although that sounds like fun!
- I wasn't pregnant.
- I never had a chest injury or lung disease.
- I had zero genetic markers.
- Plus, I was young—blebs mostly occur in people between twenty and forty.

The only profile indicator I had was that I was tall (5'11") and thin (120 pounds).

From Bad to Worse

One minute I was fine; the next, I couldn't breathe.

Talk about terrifying!

Then, in November, the frequency increased. When once the blebs had been happening monthly, it quickly became weekly, and then daily.

My local hospital wasn't equipped to handle this anymore, and, besides, I needed to have a pulmonologist present for treatment. So, Mom had to drive ninety minutes home from work to pick me up and another two hours to Nemours Children's Hospital.

I was scared.

My parents were, too.

Thanksgiving Week

It was the week before Thanksgiving. I was in Nemours. Again! No somersault dive this time.

Both lungs had collapsed, and surgeons had to insert tubes between my ribs into the space around the lungs to drain the air and allow them to re-expand. I looked like a Cyborg!

Finally, the tubes came out the day before Thanksgiving. Boy, was I happy! Not only could I breathe, but I also got to eat Thanksgiving dinner. And in our Italian family, that's not a meal you want to miss!

Surgery was twenty-five days away. The countdown had begun, and we were all on tenterhooks that my lungs would collapse.

They didn't.

However, due to a second bout with pneumonia six months prior, I was headed into surgery with my lungs weaker than ideal.

The Day of

Finally December 17, 2009, arrived. I was scheduled for surgery to remove the blebs in both lungs to stop them from collapsing. It's a minor surgery as far as surgeries go, yet it was a big deal for me.

I went in at 9:00 a.m. and was in recovery by 5:00 p.m. That's when I started hemorrhaging!

So back into surgery I went to stop the bleeding.

Later, I found out I'd hemorrhaged over two liters of blood in a few seconds. Considering that the average-sized person only has five liters of blood in their body, I'd lost nearly half within seconds!

The doctors immediately hooked me up to a cardiopulmonary bypass machine that took over the functions of my heart and lungs. Whereas my first surgery had been done laparoscopically, this was a major, open-lung emergency surgery. They cut me open from my upper right shoulder, across my back, and around my scapula.

It wasn't until after midnight that my parents could visit me in ICU. By that time, I'd been given morphine for the pain and was hooked up to all kinds of equipment.

That's when I saw them.

Angels Watching Over Me

All night, all day.
Angels watching over me, my Lord.

The lyrics to this African American spiritual were written by Otis L. McCoy, a singer-songwriter from South Carolina who published his hymn in the 1930s.[9]

Woven between his lyrics were the words to a classic children's bedtime prayer from the eighteenth century, Now I Lay Me Down to Sleep:

Now I lay me down to sleep.
Angels watching over me, my Lord.
I pray the Lord my soul to keep.
Angels watching over me.

And they were.

Lying in my ICU bed with my Christmas reindeer nestled on my chest, I thought I was dying.

That's when I saw her.

At the foot of my bed, flanked by two other spirits, stood the Archangel Gabriella. Gabriella (the feminine energy of Archangel Gabriel) emitted a white light and a warm, loving energy. She said to me:

I'm Archangel Gabriella. I'm your spirit guide. I'm going to protect you, and I know that you are going to be well taken care of.

---

9   *Singing Our Faith: A Hymnal for Young Catholics*, 2nd ed, GIA Publications, 2014.

I'm here to help you through your surgery. This is something you have to go through to get where you need to be in life.

As I drifted back to sleep, her comforting energy enveloped me. And no matter when I awoke, she was there.

So was God.

No, Not on My Watch

I wasn't raised in a religious home. Growing up, I never gave God, spirit guides, or angels much thought.

Both my parents were baptized Catholic, although they weren't practicing Catholics. However, they promised my great-grandmother I would attend CCD classes (religious education) in first grade and be confirmed in ninth grade. So, I did—hating every minute—and in the end, I still didn't really believe in anything.

Except for Gabriella.

As part of the confirmation process, I had to pick a name I wanted to have conferred upon me from one of the saints we were studying. I chose Gabriella.

And much to our family's astonishment, the Catholic Church allowed me to be confirmed with that name!

So, maybe it wasn't surprising that Archangel Gabriella appeared to me at the foot of my bed when I needed her the most.

What *was* surprising was that God did!

God's Healing Miracle

I felt God's presence before I saw him.

It was stronger than Archangel Gabriella's and of a much higher vibration. Even before I opened my eyes, I knew God was present.

Goosebumps popped on my arms, and the light emanating from God was nothing I'd seen before. God was radiating gold! And as I felt its warmth engulf me, I heard him say:

I'm here to save you, Alyssa. I'm here to answer your prayers. I'm here to perform a miracle on your lungs.

As he spoke, I felt jittery, excited, and filled with love. I intuitively knew that I was being upgraded to a higher-frequency vibration. And that this was both a healing miracle for my body and an energetic attunement for my life.

To this day, whenever I feel that jitteriness, I know God is near and I'm receiving further upgrades.

My Life Today

I'd like to say that since God's miracle, I haven't needed any more surgeries, but I have—though not on my lungs. God healed those.

What's changed is that I now have a relationship with my spirit guides, angels, and, of course, God and Archangel Gabriella. I talk to them daily, feel their presence constantly, and know, without any doubt, that there are always angels watching over me. And you.

And my mom, too.

Alyssa DiDomenico, an intuitive creator with Asperger Syndrome, crafts custom jewelry. She shares her life with parents, Anthony and Donna, along with two canine companions, Cooper, her intuitive sidekick, and Bella, who bosses everyone. Her unique perspective on the world shapes her creative journey. Her happy place is the beach.

CourageousImpact.com

ANGELS WATCHING OVER ME, TOO!

Donna DiDomenico

Alyssa, the author of the previous chapter, is not the only one with angels watching over her.

Maybe it runs in the family. Or perhaps it's because Alyssa and I are mother and daughter, and I prayed so fervently to have her and nearly lost her so many times that our angels have been working overtime keeping watch.

Either way, angels are watching over us.

And miracles abound.

For the Hundredth Time, No!

It was early April 2012, and our new bedroom furniture was arriving the next day. It had been ages since my husband Anthony and I updated our bedroom, and we were excited about our new furniture.

But first, we had to move the old furniture out to make way for the new, and some things, like my hope chest, would be going to a new home.

231

So, there I was, on my knees, cleaning it out with Alyssa in my face, screaming at me for the hundredth time to change my mind about something I'd long ago said no to.

(If you're a mother, you know what it's like having a child, even an adult one like Alyssa, on a mission to get you to change your mind —They. Never. Give. Up!)

I was busy, Alyssa was hounding me, and I was fed up.

"Alyssa, would you please just leave the room and give me some space?"

It's Just a Bump

No sooner had I spoken those words when I lost my balance, fell backward, and hit the left side of my head on the edge of the hope chest.

Ouch!

Alyssa's anger was out of control—she had yet to be diagnosed on the autism spectrum—and was threatening to kill herself because she didn't know how to process her anger. With Alyssa's life a more pressing concern than the bump on my head, we drove to the Princeton Crisis Center to get her help.

We waited over twelve hours for someone to see us. My head was pounding, so I lay down beside Alyssa on the emergency room bed, thinking that once I returned home, I'd take a Tylenol, and all would be well.

Boy, was I wrong.

Thirty Days of Hell

Over the next few days, Alyssa was evaluated and transferred to Princeton House Behavioral Health, where she was admitted for inpatient psychiatric care. It was there that she was diagnosed with Bipolar II Disorder. She was twenty-one years old.

I was a working mother, so on Monday, I returned to work at The Vitamin Shoppe in North Bergen, New Jersey, where I was the head of Learning and Development.

My daily commute was a ninety-minute drive on the New Jersey Turnpike—each way. On good days, it was a grueling commute. Doing it with a splitting headache that refused to go away, no matter how much Tylenol I popped, made it brutal.

"You need to see someone about your headaches," Anthony said more than once.

"It's just a headache!" I said dismissively equally as often.

Looking back and knowing what I know now, it's a miracle I didn't die while commuting to work.

That was miracle number one.

Popping Tylenol Like Candy

The headaches were relentless and getting worse. I was popping Tylenol Extra Strength caplets like candy.

Yet I still didn't go to see a doctor.

Silly me.

But I had my reasons!

First, I had completely forgotten about hitting my head on the hope chest. And considering all that was happening with Alyssa, a headache seemed minor.

Plus, by now, I was thinking I had a sinus infection. No biggie. There was no reason to take off work for a sinus infection that would eventually go away, right?

Wrong!

The pain became unbearable, forcing me to cave in and go to urgent care one night after work.

"Donna, this isn't a sinus infection," the doctor said.

"Okay. What is it?"

"We need you to go to the emergency room for a CT scan."

"Nope, I don't have time for that," I said, hopping off the table.

"Well, at least go see your Primary Care Physician (PCP) as soon as possible," the doctor urged.

"Okay."

A week later, I went.

Hardheaded or Hard Head?

"Donna," my PCP said, "You need a CT scan."

"All right."

The next day, I went to work. (When will I learn to listen to my doctor?)

Three days later, I had the CT scan done at a radiology center. The radiologist called my PCP, who called me at the center and told me the news I never expected to hear:

"Donna, you have an acute subdural hematoma (SDH) and require immediate surgery."

"No, I don't," I stubbornly protested.

"Yes, you do."

"Because of the magnitude of your injury, an ambulance will take you to Capital Health Regional Health Center in Trenton, New Jersey."

"Oh no, that's not happening."

"It's a state law, Donna," she explained.

I thought about it for a moment, looking for a solution I could live with.

"How about if I call Anthony to come pick me up, and he drives me to the hospital? Will that work?"

So I did, and we drove straight to the emergency room entrance.

There, the neurosurgeon met us and said in a tone that left no room for any ambiguity:

"Donna, it's a miracle you're even functioning."

That was miracle number two.

He continued: "With what's happening inside your brain, you should be experiencing blindness, slurred speech, and difficulty walking! But the fact that you're arguing with me suggests that we need to conduct an MRI in the morning to gather more information."

(Okay, maybe I was being a bit hardheaded about this.)

After the MRI, he delivered another shocker: "Donna, your MRI revealed that your brain has been forced into the right corner of your skull because of the pressure building up due to the significant bleeding. It's a miracle you're still alive!"

Another miracle—number three.

There's No Way You're Going to Shave My Head!

It was the day before Mother's Day, and while my neurosurgeon was explaining what the operation would entail, my mind was preoccupied with a seemingly trivial concern—my hair.

"You're not shaving my head," I firmly asserted.

"Donna, you're undergoing *brain* surgery," he emphasized.

"I understand, but I'm going to Italy with Anthony and Alyssa in two weeks. I can't go with half my head shaved!"

"Donna, you're not going anywhere in two weeks except to bed."

"We'll see about that."

He chuckled.

Defying the Odds

The neurosurgeon took his scalpel and made a long incision across the left side of my head, down the back, curving around to the front and ending above my ear. Then he peeled back the left side of my scalp to expose my brain, drained the clotted blood, and cauterized the wound that had been hemorrhaging for the past thirty days.

Before reattaching my scalp, the surgical team briefly woke me up to see if I could blink my eyes and move my toes and fingers. To their relief and amazement, I could!

Miracle number four.

Statistically, I had defied the odds. The mortality rate for patients with an acute SDH ranges from 50 to 90 percent, with only 20 to 30 percent expected to recover full or partial brain function.

To compound matters, I was a hardheaded fifty-two-year-old and had waited a month to get treatment.

The fact that I emerged from this ordeal with full functionality was nothing short of a miracle. Just like

Alyssa, who was hemorrhaging on the recovery table and "should have" died.

And that was miracle number five.

My Mother's Day Gift

The day after Mother's Day, I insisted that the hospital release me—I just wanted to get home and sleep in my own bed. While my doctor was busy ensuring I could navigate steps, speak in complete sentences, and see without my vision blurring, I noticed there were no mirrors in my room.

How come there aren't any mirrors? Do I look that bad?

As the nurse wheeled me to the elevator, I saw myself in the reflective doors for the first time and gasped.

"Oh my God!"

"Don't worry," the nurse said soothingly, "I'll part your hair on the other side, and no one will know the difference."

And just like that, she flipped my hair over to the other side.

Vanity restored!

But the story doesn't end there.

Five Miracles

Looking back over the events, it's truly astounding. From bumping my head against the hope chest in early April to my release from the hospital following brain surgery the day after Mother's Day, I'd experienced five miracles in thirty days. And I could no longer ignore three things:

1. It was clear that the biggest miracle I'd been given that Mother's Day was the gift of life—I'd been deliberately set upon a new path. Although I didn't know what that path was, I accepted that it would reveal itself, and that was enough at the time.
2. The other thing that was impossible to ignore was that something beyond the ordinary had intervened on my behalf—there's just no other way to explain why I was still here—and it was God.
3. Finally, angels were watching over me. And I know, without a doubt, that I would not be alive today without them.

Through my journey and that of Alyssa's, I now know this to be true: Angels are actively involved in our lives. They protect us during times of danger and offer solace during our moments of despair. They are here to support, intervene, and assist in miraculous ways.

Keep an eye out for your angels. They're watching over us all.

Donna DiDomenico is the owner of Be the Difference, which redefines leadership for current and future leaders. She offers a unique, intuitive approach  to shift from command and control to inclusive, authentic leadership. Donna cherishes life with her husband, Anthony, their daughter, Alyssa, and their two inspiring dogs, Cooper and Bella.

BeTheDifference.global

Susan L. Reid collaborated with many of our authors, helping them bring their inspirational stories to life.

In the realm where words transcend expression, Susan is a highly sought-after intuitive ghostwriter inspiriting and inspiring greatness in authors. Specializing in the self-help, entrepreneurship, and spirituality genres, she crafts narratives that resonate with transformative energy, aligning authors with their readers in a way that surpasses conventional storytelling.

Susan's expertise lies not just in the art of words but in the art of connection—an alchemy that transforms stories into experiences.

For those yearning to elevate their narratives, Susan invites you to connect with her at Susan@Alkamae.com and embark on a literary adventure where what lies beyond the words truly matters.

Success is assured,
Greatness is,
Beauty surrounds, and
All is well.

Alkamae.com

Meet **Denise Sutter** of Eden Soul Designs, creator of the mandala that appears on the cover of this book. Denise describes herself as an energetic artist who stumbled upon her extraordinary talent during a transformative retreat at the mystical Mount Shasta. There, she received a divine calling to do pictorial readings, blending intricate symbols with profound messages for those in attendance.

Upon returning home, Denise extended her pictorial readings to her clients, effortlessly incorporating them into her Reiki and Heart Path sessions. However, it didn't stop there. And channeling her artistic spirit to capture the essence of her day soon became a daily soul-nurturing ritual. These nightly drawings soon evolved into breathtaking art and mandalas, revealing her burgeoning psychic abilities.

In the wake of her mother's unexpected passing in October 2022, Denise's art took on a new dimension. Her doodling evolved into more detailed works of art and mandalas adorned with intricate symbols and vibrant colors using metallic ink on black paper. What began as a personal healing journey as she grieved the loss of her mother blossomed into a transformative energy therapy practice.

Today, Denise invokes healing, activation, and soul remembrance through her energetic art that she channels and crafts into personal and business mandalas for individuals and groups.

Her art exudes hope and a deep sense of returning to one's true self.

Denise is thrilled and honored to contribute her inspirational story and art to this book. To explore more of her creations and connect with the energy she channels, visit https://EdenSoulDesigns.wordpress.com.

Printed in the USA
CPSIA information can be obtained
at www.ICGtesting.com
JSHW050211140524
62892JS00011B/7